From Glory to Holy

From Glory to Holy

An Inner Life Journey through the
Renewed Temple of Prophet Ezekiel and
Spiritual Doctrines of St. John of the Cross

Sinimol Mathew

Christian World Imprints

First Published in 2020 by

Christian World Imprints
Christian Publishing & Books from India
C-3, Wazirpur Industrial Area
Delhi-110052
cwidelhi2017@gmail.com
www.ChristianWorldImprints.com
Phone: +91 11 41526079

ISBN: 978-93-5148-436-3

Printed in India.

Dedicated to
Jesus Our Saviour
Who planted me in a very fertile land of spiritual
nourishments and in Whom
I remain with all.

Contents

Acknowledgements

Our God surely deserves and desires the first fruit of everything and I really confess the great power of God in this work and thank Almighty God for all the heavenly aid in being with me and completing this work. My sincere and deep felt thanks to all the respected authorities who are in the administration and for providing all the support and encouragements in my studies, very specially, Rev. Dr. Tomy Paul Kakkatuthadathil, the President of Pontifical Institute Aluva for supporting me with much concern; Rev. Dr. Joy Arackal, the Vice-President and the Director of M.Th. I also remember with gratitude all my former authorities who accepted me in the very beginning of my studies with very simple and humble approaches that dispelled all my academic fear. And it was God's great mercy that He gifted me with an efficient guide; Rev. Dr. Joseph Oliapurath who is also the head of the department of Spiritual Theology. Besides all his busy schedules and responsibilities, he has really worked hard with me for the perfection and completion of this work. I wouldn't have been reaching this stage of providence in absence of his guidance. I extend him all my gratitude for his very precious and graceful support in imparting scientific skills, guidance provided with a prayerful spirit and corrections with divine wisdom that imparted from the very beginning until its completion now. Also, I express my heartfelt thanks to my readers, Rev. Dr. Antony Valunkal, whose valuable suggestions right from the schema reading has helped me to enter into a novel thinking and Rev. Dr. Sugun Leon, whose words of appreciation and constructive suggestions has helped me to make this work perfect and beautiful. I also extend my heartfelt gratitude to all the professors who helped me in acquiring the spiritual growth and knowledge in theological study as well as our parish priest Rev. Fr. Jose Cholikara whose fraternal care, consideration and support remained with us throughout. Here, I record my thanks to all my companions with deep sentiments of gratitude. The cherishing memories of our classroom studies, support and encouragements keeps all of them ever remembered in my prayers. My heartfelt thanks to all the office staffs whose support, concern and good will has supported me alot in completing my work. Also, I thank my beloved families, parents and all my dear ones in facilitating my study with much support and very specially my children and life partner; Mr. Shenny Joseph Kolenchery whose renunciations, support, hardships, sufferings and prayers has helped me a lot in perfecting and completing it. With one hand alone, nothing is gained here. Though last, with lasting love I remember all our well-wishers and all the respected hands that supported me with needed requirements such as books and materials, prayers and all other forms of help.

Abbreviations

A	-	The Ascent of Mount Carmel
D N	-	The Dark Night
L.F.	-	The Living Flame of Love
S.C.	-	The Spiritual Canticle
C.C.C.	-	Catechism of the Catholic Church
Cf.	-	confer
et.al	-	et.alii (and others)
vol.	-	Volume, Volumes

General Introduction

In our life journey most often our focus is on what is visible, communicated or experienced by the exterior senses. Our craving and quest in life is centred on what is perishable and momentary. We mislay our time and energy, days and years for profits that are worthless and perishing. Human lives and relations end up on things and ideas that have neither temporal nor eternal values. The reason behind is the lack of true knowledge and understanding of oneself. He fails to ask the questions who he is, what the meaning of his life and existence, what one's relationship with the universe and other human beings and so on.When one does not think of these questions, one may not be able to possess an experience of the supernatural or God. Here the words of prophet Hosea "my people are destroyed for lack of knowledge; because you have rejected knowledge" (Hos 4:6) becomes true.

Privation of the knowledge of God is the cause of indifference[1] in every aspect of human life and relations. There is a fast growing trend towards modern advanced facilities for every immediate requirement and also an overdependence on material and virtual aspects which makes human beings to forget of his birth as beginning to eternity. This tendency keeps persons veiled from the real track of self-knowledge and taking refuge in God.[2] It is the convictions in life

1 Pius X, "Acerbo Nimis", in Vincent A. Yzermans (ed.), *All Things in Christ*, The New-Man Press, Westminster 1954) p. 47.

2 Kieran Kavanaugh, *John of the Cross; Doctor of Light and Love*, (The Crossroad Publishing Company, New York, 1999) p. 64.

which enable persons to begin their journey towards the truth in life. It is this same conviction that makes one to tread the journey towards God and slowly comes to hold faith in Him.[3] There is an unending quest in man towards the Creator, with an open door of reason that changes one's mind.[4] This gradual process of growth in the knowledge of God can help to proceed in the knowledge of self and at the end, the journey may reach to its summit of holiness in a stage where "nothing" is his requirement (cf. Job 42:5-6), as God has even emptied Himself in Christ.

It is at this point that the temple vision of Ezekiel becomes important for a new understanding. Ezekiel began his journey with the manifestation of the glory of Yahweh in a remote place of exile[5] but ends with the vision of God in a "very holy" place in the temple, causing to his people an integral self-awareness which leads to a deep sense of shame where their whole life is illumined and revealed critically.[6] Though, this vision never worked out as a blueprint for an actual temple,[7] numerous are the ones who could find a holy temple within themselves with a glorious indwelling of God in them. This aspect is very evident in Ezekiel 12:3-4 when God says "Therefore, son of man, prepare for yourself an exile's baggage, and go into exile by day in their sight; you shall go like an exile from your place to another place in their sight. Perhaps they will understand, though they are a rebellious house. You shall bring out your baggage by day in their sight, as baggage for exile; and you shall go forth yourself at evening in their sight, as men do who must go into exile." This was the change that God demanded from Israel when He asked the prophet symbolically to pack an exile's bundle.

---

3 Cf. Paul VI, "Preparation for Christmas", in *The Teachings of Pope Paul VI*, (Libreria Editrice Vaticana, 1976) 144.

4 Paul VI, "Preparation for Christmas", p. 144.

5 Walther Zimmerli, *Ezekiel 1A, Commentary on the Book of the Prophet Ezekiel* (Philadelphia, Fortress Press, 1977) 53.

6 Walther Zimmerli, *Ezekiel 2, A Commentary on the Book of the Prophet Ezekiel*, (Philadelphia Fortress Press, 1983) pp. 418-420.

7 Lawrence Boadt, "Ezekiel", in Brown R E., Fitzmyer J. A.– Murphy R. E. (ed.), *The New Jerome Biblical Commentary* (Bangalore: Theological Publications in India, 2004) p. 326.

John of the Cross is one of the saintliest souls in the Catholic Church of the 16th century gifted with experience of God's indwelling. His life is the response of the whole mystery of this glorious indwelling and self-emptying of God in human soul through Christ. St. John of the Cross narrates in his journey of the soul the meeting of God in a similar departure from an exilic life.[8] In the narration of the temple vision of Ezekiel one could see glimpses of historical contexts and external factors contributed to narrate such a vision. But a deep contextual reading of the vision narrative and the various contexts of the book of Ezekiel gives us the impression that the temple vision is not only a simple narration of the vision of the prophet but it also conveys an inner meaning in the life context of each individual of Israel and also the community as a whole. The intention of the temple vision is the reconstruction of the community and also for learning to transform each individual's wretched situations and humiliations to the glory and to the final summation to the holy of holies. In the narration of the ascending spiritual journey of St. John of the cross, it is purely an inner state of human soul through a step by step process ascending to the most holy One. Even though there is no similarity in its historical sense of both the contexts, one could attribute its transforming process into a spiritual dimension. In the case of Israel, Israel as a nation, as a community and as individuals and in St. John of the Cross in a given context of time and space proposes the need of inner transformation in the community level and in the personal level. In both of these experiences the outcome is a change that leads to the true knowledge, a total transformation of the soul and body; a knowledge in the understanding of God, of oneself and one's brethren. It is also getting away from all self - seeking of the intellect, will and memory that may impede the divine union.[9] A leaving or going out of oneself is

8 John of the Cross, The Ascend of Mount Carmel, l. l, in Keiran Kavanaugh, Otilio Rodriguez (tr.), *St. John of the Cross, Collected Works* (Carmel International Publishing House, Trivandrum, Kerala, 2006) p. 73.

9 Norbert Cummins, *An Introduction to St. John of the Cross*, (Darlington Carmel, [Private circulation only]) p. 80.

not a flight that isolate oneself from others, but to know better, and for a transformed expression towards the other as a spiritual being.[10]

The transformation of the body and soul occur, also depending on many factors such as the mind, will, emotions and circumstances. Though it is the mind that can be changed faster than changing one's circumstances, in reality, it is for the change of mind that one takes more time and energy. As one sees in the parable of the sower (Mt 13: 4-8) the sower sows the same seeds, but the growth depends upon the receptivity of the ground. In the same way, in human persons this change always depends upon the nature of the mind and soul as well as the awareness and the degree of knowledge and a union based on experience.[11] What has to be changed and has to be formed within us is the mentality or mind. The human intellect is the guide in this journey of knowledge.[12]

So, the revitalization into a Christian mentality[13] is accentuated through the continuous transformation and the renewal of our mind. Here the words of St. Paul, "Do not be conformed to this world but be transformed by the renewal of your mind, that you may prove what is the will of God, what is good and acceptable and perfect" (Rom 12:2) becomes important and it is this change we need to focus. Everything is first fashioned and formed in the mind (cf. Sir 37:16-18). As man's goodness consists in interior acts,[14] it is very important for the fruitful flowing out, in the beginning an inward journey with intellect as guide, along with the divine knowledge as a companion.[15] It is with this aim the study on the growth of the inner life of the person according to St. John of the Cross is selected in relation to the temple vision of the Prophet Ezekiel where we are

---

10 G. Benny Koottanal, "Salesian Eucharistic Theology Anthropological Perspectives", in *Indian Journal of Spirituality*, (2012) V. XXV, 2, pp. 133-135.

11 G. Benny KoottanaL, "Salesian Eucharistic Theology Anthropological Perspectives", p. 136.

12 Pius X, "Acerbo Nimis", p. 47.

13 PAUL VI, "The Unity of the Church", in *The Teachings of Pope Paul VI*, (Libreria Editrice Vaticana, 1976) p. 12.

14 Kieran Kavanaugh, Otilio Rodriguez, (tr.), *St. John of the Cross, Collected Works* (Carmel International Publishing House, Trivandrum, Kerala, 2006) p. 29.

15 Pius X, "Acerbo Nimis, p. 47.

introduced to an inward journey by ascending through a ladder that is wisdom and divine knowledge. This journey is to a new centre where one encounter with a proper balancing,[16] in terms with the known and unknown realities, visible and invisible experiences of life. As the journey proceeds we come across different areas of our inner life.

Objective of the Study

This is a general study on the inner life of human person as an interpretative journey by using the structural analysis of Man according to St. John of the Cross with special reference to the vision of the New Temple of Prophet Ezekiel and its spiritual explanations. Faith graces the human mind, Hope graces the repentant heart and Love graces human decisions and all these forms of created grace transform the natural elements that structure human experience. Experience grows through transmutation and it occurs every time with a new evaluation, interaction or tendency which is integrated into a developing experience so as to change its constitutive relational structure with new complexity to human experience.[17] This study will be focussing on this transmuting grace and how we are created anew in Christ. Here, also the concept of St. Paul human body as God's temple (1Cor 3:16) shall be considered. The concept that human person is the 'living and transformed temple' is the supernatural dignity of every person. A perfect life in Christ is a life as glorious and holy temple where the Spirit of God take abode and where the life-giving fruits are produced throughout the year disregarding any season. The habit of seeing the hand of God in all things with peaceful equanimity helped St. John of the Cross to make proper judgment with right remedy. Bible was the book he

---

16 Ezek 41:3-4; JAMES ARRAJ, *St. John of the Cross and Dr. C.G. Jung*, (Inner Growth Books, USA, 1988) p. 13.

17 L. Donald Gelpi, *Charism and Sacrament*, (SPCK, London 1977) p. 69.

cherished most of all,[18] and the chief source of his writings.[19] This is a small attempt to enter into this cherishing grace of the Word of God and to recognize how Christ became the central focus in reaching this deepest centre-God. For this, an analytical and interpretative study with the support of preliminary sources is made.

Sources of the Work

Primary Sources here are the Bible and the four major doctrinal writings of St. John of the Cross: The Ascent of Mount Carmel, The Dark Night, The Spiritual Canticle, The Living Flame of Love. The secondary sources are other books, studies and writings available on the specified theme of the primary sources.

Scope and Relevance of the Study

The completeness of human life comprises an integral growth of body, mind and soul. But it is the formation of the mind or the duration of one's process of knowing through reflection that serves to accommodate the world of sense or body to the spirit, where a mysterious and new experience begins.[20] Change in one's thinking is more preferred than changing one's behaviour.[21] It happens when one examines his or her life with the recognition of a mystical dimension along with the biblical revelation. Eventually, we reach to a perfect path of development in all human aspects such as physical, psychological and spiritual. Another aspect is reading the signs of life from the given circumstances as the soul pass through the transition stages: its transmuting journey to the holy mount, to a new centre of

---

18 Kieran Kavanaugh, Otilio Rodriguez, (tr.), St. John of the Cross, Collected Works (Carmel International Publishing House, Trivandrum, Kerala, 2006) p. 32.

19 Kieran Kavanaugh, Otilio Rodriguez (tr.), St. John of the Cross, Collected Works (Carmel International Publishing House, Trivandrum, Kerala, 2006) p. 45.

20 James Arraj, *St John of the Cross and Dr. C. G. Jung*, p. 57.

21 Antony John, *Family Counselling*, (Anugraha Publications, Dindigul, 2005) p. 12.

the soul or self.[22] Here, in the journey, our intellect may be in a dark den with all the aridity the soul can face with by the interference of the world, flesh and devil which are qualified as three blind men by St. John of the Cross.[23] Along with this a guiding light – the mind of Christ will be lit within, as the attitude of Christ will measure the altitude of our life.[24]

The natural human tendency is to look at the other and correct the other. It may be easy to correct oneself than correcting the other. But we are more disposed to changing the other than changing oneself. As usually says, the faculties of our self may always blind us with a mind of 'I'm right and you are not right'. Christ's mind is always an invitation to analyse oneself with every moment of life: "We destroy arguments and every proud obstacle raised up against the knowledge of God, and we take every thought captive to obey Christ" (cf. 2 Cor 10:4-5).

It is only the one who realizes one's own dignity and value of soul can respond to the growing need of respect for human rights.[25] There is a call within all to find this hidden value amidst every experiences of life and every person sincerely open to the truth and goodness, by the light of reason and the hidden action of grace, can come to recognize this sacred value of human life from its very beginning until its end.[26]

This research study is an attempt to gain a profound inspiration to live a life of holiness that Prophet Ezekiel designed through his temple structure and St. John of the Cross taught through his divine wisdom consistent with power that purifies and love that unite oneself to God.

---

22 James Arraj, *St John of the Cross and Dr. C.G. Jung*, p. 57; John Of The Cross, The Living Flame of Love, 1:9, in Keiran Kavanaugh, Otilio Rodriguez (tr.), *St. John of the Cross, Collected Works* (Carmel International Publishing House, Trivandrum, Kerala, 2006).

23 John of the Cross, L F, 3:29.

24 John of the Cross, L F, 4:7-8.

25 John Paul II, "Ecclesia in America", in *Pope John Paul II Apostolic Exhortations*, (Carmel International Publishing House, Trivandrum, 2005) p. 387.

26 John Paul II, "Evangelium Vitae", in *Pope John Paul II Encyclicals*, (Carmel International Publishing House, Trivandrum, 2005) p. 240.

Methodology and Procedure

There is no quest for truth in any field without presuppositions or postulations. They determine the nature of the procedures that are followed in it. The methodology applied for this study would be more of analytical with supporting texts from the Scripture and the doctrines of John of the Cross and other writings that are parallel or comparative to the selected theme. Spiritual application of symbolic materials, words, and also actions used in the prescribed texts after verifying the historical factors is also made use of. This study will be an analysis on the human soul that ought to be the living temple of God, based on the writings of St. John of the Cross and also a spiritual reflective outlook on the Temple vision of Ezekiel as a support in this interpretative journey. For this, the following procedure has been adopted:

In the First chapter, body that rooted in the Spirit is the theme that will be discussed. Body with five senses has its own relevance in the life of a spiritual person. Just as the holy of holies is called the throne and foot stool of Yahweh, the body is the residing place of the soul and the soul serves through body. This chapter will analyse the structure of human person who leads the spiritual journey according to the spirituality of St. John of the Cross.

First chapter is almost concerned with the relevant participants of the inner journey of human soul according to the spirituality of St. John of the Cross. The main participants in this journey are the *exterior faculties* and the *interior faculties* of the human self.[27] There will be a structural analysis of the notion of soul according to St. John of the Cross which are extracted from his treatises. His division of soul is in two main parts: the *lower part* and the *higher part* or the sensory, and the spiritual.[28] The sense organs of the body also fall

---

27 E. W. Trueman Dicken, *The Crucible of Love, A Study of the Mysticism of St. Teresa of Jesus and St. John of the Cross*, (Sheed and Ward, New York,1963) pp. 327-51; Eulogio Pacho, *The Art of Reaching God According to St. John of the Cross*, Augustine Mulloor (tr.), (Jyothir Dhara Publications, Kalamassery 1990) pp. 82-95; Gregory D'souza, *Contemplative Formation*, (Dhyanavana Publications, Bangalore, 2013) pp. 71-117.

28 Kieran Kavanaugh, Otilio Rodriguez, (tr.), "Introduction to the Ascend –Dark Night" in *St. John of the Cross, Collected Works*, p. 47.

under this division of the lower part of the soul because according to St. John of the Cross, the functional aspect of the body rest upon the governing principles of the soul.[29] The sensory parts contain the external parts, the five sense organs along with the reduced inner faculties; the fantasy and the imagination. Instead of calling it body, this part the Saint refers as the Lower part of the soul. The whole force of balanced life conforms and unifies the sensual part with the rational and natural to the supernatural.[30] The higher part consists of the other faculties of the interior senses; the Memory, Intellect and Will, and he refers them as the higher part of the soul.[31] As our thought is necessarily composed of intuition and sense experience, memory lies in our association of images with sensations and of sensations with ideas. It is incomplete unless it results from both these elements.[32] Hence, the steps of renewing memory in the journey is a two-edged process of purgation.

The intellect reaches its perfection through a growth in the divine knowledge and continues its journey through illumination. The unitive ways are controlled by the Will where the will direct all the faculties, passions, and appetites toward God, turning them away from all that is not God, and preserving its strength for God, to love Him with all its might. There will be an analysis of the relevance of our daily life examining on the basis of the four passions that controls the Will. Such soul will be a living temple and a new temple with a new heart. Here, one is able to enter into the centre of the soul, the deepest centre-God.[33]

---

29 E. W. Trueman Dicken, *The Crucible of Love, A Study of the Mysticism of St. Teresa of Jesus and St. John of the Cross,* p. 329.

30 Eulogio Pacho, *The Art of Reaching God According to St. John of the Cross,* p. 92.

31 Kieran Kavanaugh, Otilio Rodriguez, (tr.), "Introduction to the Ascend –Dark Night" in *St. John of the Cross, Collected Works,* p. 47; E.W. Trueman Dicken, *The Crucible of Love, A Study of the Mysticism of St. Teresa of Jesus and St. John of the Cross,* 327-351.

32 Antonio Rosmini, Denis Cleary, Watson Terence, (tr.), *Development of the Human Soul,* (Rosmini House, Durham,1989) V. 2, p. 160.

33 John of the Cross, "The Living Flame of Love", in Keiran Kavanaugh, Otilio Rodriguez (tr.), *St. John of the Cross, Collected Works* (Carmel International Publishing House, Trivandrum, Kerala, 2006) p. 583.

The Second Chapter focuses on the main structure of the new temple of Prophet Ezekiel and reflecting on the spaces, steps, procedures in the temple, direction, etc., with a spiritual explanation in the light of the spirituality of St. John of the Cross. Defending the uniqueness and authenticity of the temple vision of prophet Ezekiel, this study will be delimiting to the moral and spiritual aspects of the temple vision where it supports the inner journey of the soul to the high mountain of perfection. This chapter will also be an attempt to enter into the wisdom of St. John of the Cross in the reflection of Scripture.[34]

Here, there shall be the analysis of the question of, how and where a temple is designed and formed and how its entire plan and ordinances can be observed rather than built. In Ezekiel 43:10 the words "and you, son of man, describe to the house of Israel the temple and its appearance and plan, that they may be ashamed of their iniquities" implies the symbolic nature of its presentation. This may be more of a reflective analysis with each part of the previous chapter and discerning how it can be a living temple - the human being (1Cor. 6:19, 2Cor. 6:16) when it is synthesized in the light of the spirituality of St. John of the Cross.

The Third Chapter is an entry into the beauty of God in Christ in order to love Him. True love gives rise to a whole new dimension of knowing: a knowing of God through Christ[35] where God's perfect consolation is present in every need.[36] The real love and joy of life, embodied in recognizing the unconditional and reconciling love in Jesus regardless of one's own worth[37] is the core focus of this chapter. This chapter invokes to a sharing of the gift of love by entering into

34 Kieran Kavanaugh, "Faith and the Experience of God in the University town of Baeza", in *Carmelite Studies, John of the Cross: Conferences and Essays by Members of the Institute of Carmelite Studies and Others*, Payne Steven (ed.), (ICS Publications, Washington, D.C. 1992) p. 57.

35 John of the Cross, "The Spiritual Canticle" in Keiran Kavanaugh, Otilio Rodriguez (tr.), *St. John of the Cross, Collected Works* (Carmel International Publishing House, Trivandrum, Kerala, 2006) p. 549.

36 Ross Collings, *John of the Cross, The Way of the Christian Mystics*, (The Liturgical Press, Collegeville, Minnesota, 1990) p. 153.

37 Ross Collings, *John of the Cross, The Way of the Christian Mystics*, p. 153.

the sacramental life with an inner experience of life in the Trinity with a personal understanding of one's own life in God's love.[38] There is an invitation to withdraw our affections from all in order to find God in the centre of our life.[39] This chapter will lead to an insight into the directing ways of God through all the winds and voices of life and find God in the 'city of self', where everything done and lived for the glory of God.[40] Though in faith we are able to reach God, the inability to keep this faith in its discretion at all times is very strong. But the sacramental grace that we receive at all times is also very tangible and clear even when our faith, hope and love are feeble.[41] This will be a grace journey where our simple knowledge of Jesus Christ is comprehended rather than fragmented from our daily living.[42]

---

38 Ross Collings, *John of the Cross, The Way of the Christian Mystics*, p. 155.

39 P. Richard Hardy, "Embodied love in John of the Cross", in *Carmelite Studies, John of the Cross: Conferences and Essays by Members of The Institute of Carmelite Studies and Others*, Payne Steven (ed.), (ICS Publications, Washington, D.C., 1992) p. 129.

40 Kevin Culligan, "Qualities of A Good Guide: Spiritual Direction in John of the Cross's Letters", in *Carmelite Studies, John of the Cross: Conferences and Essays by Members of The Institute of Carmelite Studies and Others*, Payne Steven (ed.), (ICS Publications, Washington, D.C., 1992) p. 70.

41 John of the Cross, in Keiran Kavanaugh, Otilio Rodriguez (tr.), *Collected Works,* p. 513.

42 Denis Read, "John of the Cross for Carpenters: The Ordinary way of the Dark Night of Faith", in *Carmelite Studies, John of the Cross: Conferences and Essays by Members of The Institute of Carmelite Studies and Others*, Payne Steven (ed.), (ICS Publications, Washington, D.C.,1992) p. 88.

Chapter 1

STRUCTURE OF HUMAN IN ST. JOHN OF THE CROSS

Introduction

Our life on earth is a partaking in Christ's glorious power (cf. Col 1:11) and a sharing in God's holiness (cf. Mt 5:48). When the life on earth begins, it begins as the beginning of a journey towards God with a constant seeking, knowing and loving Him with an integral self.[43] It continues whole through the life knowingly or unknowingly. Wholeness or integrity consists of the growth in the realm of body, mind, and soul, depending on one's strength (cf. Mk 12:30). Action is always the creation of energy. God's love and grace is this energy and strength that is always productive, dynamic and at work. The Body acts when the mind or heart commands to do or act. It always works depending on the inspiration and inclinations of the heart and mind. Therefore, the inner meaning of the body is its psyche. An action becomes a meaningful one when it is performed consciously. Heart alone cannot work; mind alone cannot work but the work becomes perfect when it is brought forth into a visible action through

---

43 *Catechism of the Catholic Church*, "Prologue", para. 1, Libreria Editrice Vaticana, (Image Doubleday, New York, 1995) p. 9.

the physical body and also according to the command or decision of a conscious mind and will. Hence, these three faculties of the body are very much inter linked and inter dependent to construct a meaningful action. Throughout the writings of John of the Cross, this integral aspects of human self is well knit and manifested.

Finite becomes infinite when it is in God or done with a Divine mind. God's Hand is the symbol of His presence, love and providence. Recognizing this divine grace in the form of divine will or work in our natural realm and transforming it to the supernatural is the core of John's teachings. But, this hand of God he never sought in an unusual or extra-ordinary way. According to him man perfects himself in conformity with the human nature by starting from the lowest and exterior to what is higher and interior.[44] In this chapter shall try to bring out a vivid picture of this integral self of human soul according to the spirituality of John of the Cross.

1.1. Structure of Man According to St. John of the Cross

Often in Indian philosophy, consciousness is thought to be the factor that transcends the biological and psychological factors which make up individual human being.[45] Though similar is the outcome, for John, this transcendency is achieved not through any extra ordinary way but through perfecting the natural to the supernatural with the support of divine grace or presence within. By this one reaches to the inmost centre or consciousness and comes out with a new self. Human life is consisted with elements (cf. 1 Cor 15:35 ff.) that are solid, visible or perishable; abstract, invisible and imperishable; Eternal and immortal. Similarly, the structure of Man in John falls under three parts. They are: (i) Lower Part of the Soul:[46] Body – With its sensory organs along with the reduced inner faculties; the fantasy and the imagination. (ii) Higher Part of the Soul:[47] Higher

44 Eulogio Pacho, *The Art of Reaching God According to St. John of the Cross, pp. 117-18; C. C.C,* "Prologue", para.1. p. 9.

45 Ninian Smart, "Hinduism" Philip L. Quinn, Charles Taliaferro (ed.) *A Companion to Philosophy of Religion,* (Blackwell Publishers, Oxford, 2000), p. 8.

46 Peter Chakiath, *The Art of Unveiling the Spirit,* (Carmel International Publishing House, Trivandrum, 2015), p. 74.

47 Peter Chakiath, *The Art of Unveiling the Spirit,* p. 74.

part is divided into three as: the (a) Intellect (b) the Memory (c) the Will. (iii) The Centre of the Soul.

According to the anatomy of the soul by John; intellect, memory and will in human person are best examples of a world of communion within the person for an unending discussion with three in one. In creation, there was a process of confirmation that God saw everything which He created and found were good (Gen 1:4, 10, 12, 18, 21). And it is also important to think that the real confirmation is the affirmation of one's conscience or spirit. Hence the word of God says; "and heed the counsel of your own heart, for no one is more faithful to you than it is" (Sir 37:13). This means that the will and true conscience of a person is in conformity with the will of God and what comes from the true conscience is affirmable. Therefore, the following part will be an analysis of the human structure with its various faculties and their unique functions in perfecting the soul throughout its life journey in the manner John analyses it.

1.1.1. Lower Part of the Soul

John calls the body as the lower part of the Soul. Body with its five senses has its own relevance in the life of a spiritual person. In the temple the holy of holies is called the throne and foot stool of Yahweh. Similarly, the body is the residing place of the soul and the soul serves through body (Ezek. 43:7). When the body is seen as a residing place of the soul, it enhances the importance of the body of a person who leads the spiritual journey or an inward journey and provides an added meaning where one may find a God who empties Himself in the body in order to get a glorified body to share His bliss at our every need.[48] In Christian spirituality, there is great effect for physical suffering because it is the way of following Christ. Christ suffered in his body and it was salvific. It is through a physical body that soul gets matured in life and love. John presents and explains human self with the imagery of watery lands. In his imagery there are two watery lands. One is the lower watery land i.e., the lower part of the soul. The other is the upper watery land i.e., the higher part of

48 Daniel Acharuparambil, "Advaita mysticism vis-a-vis the teaching of St. John of the Cross", in Panakal Justin (ed.), *St. John of the Cross, Studies on his life, doctrine and Time*, (Jyothir Dhara Publications, Kalamassery, 1991) p. 104.

the soul.[49] He brings it out with a lively example from the book of Joshua where a good prayer of Achsah as she was sent to a dry land. "Grant me a blessing! As the land you have given me is the Negeb, give me springs of water too! So, Caleb gave her what she wanted, the upper springs and the lower springs" (Josh 15:19). Comparing to the heavenly bliss, life on earth is a deprivation. Yet in a life in the grace, gifts and fruits of the Holy Spirit makes our exterior and interior senses as springs of living water. For John of the Cross "man" or "person" is substituted with "soul". The use of this term is more apt for conveying his message of perfecting and orienting the natural structure of man with the supernatural realm by penetrating into the very basic structure of human person.[50]

i. Body with its sensory organs

For John the sensory organs of the body come in the lower part of the soul, because as mentioned before, according to him, the functional aspect of the body rest upon the governing principles of the soul. He states that the soul possesses no means other than the senses, in order to perceive what is commanded to it. The sensory parts contain the external organs, the five sense organs along with the reduced inner faculties like the fantasy and the imagination. In the analysis of John with the spiritual ambient the 'lower part of the soul' consisted with five senses and they are the gateways for inflowing information into the interior faculties from the outer world and sending out the same from the interior faculties to the outer world. Here it is good to note that the five senses of which John speaks actually is in direct relationship with the material. But he calls it in the grade the lower part of the soul. So, from the very fact of presenting it in this way implies that even the senses and the material part is the first step in the movement towards the interior or towards the spiritual. But, being in constant touch with the outer world, they get the chance of being stumbled by the worldly pleasures and evil inclinations.

---

49 John of the Cross, L.F, *The Collected Works*, p. 617.

50 Eulogio Pacho, *The Art of Reaching God According to St. John of the Cross*, pp. 86-90.

Hence, this part provides a small analysis on the need of making them disciplined and free from such evil inclinations.

The five sense organs: While referring the five sensory organs (eyes, ears, nose, tongue and skin) John speaks of the importance of purification of senses in order to enter into the dark night.[51] He says that the soul through original sin is a captive in the mortal body, subject to passions and natural appetites. The soul is to be released from this prison without hindrance from the jailers. A life filled with grace is necessary to release the soul from this bondage.[52] In order to be released, one must journey through an experience similar that of one dark 'night'. This night is also divided into three parts just as the natural night.

In the first part of the night the person passes through the sensory part of the soul by casting out all strange gods that are alien affections and attachments that are not divine by disciplining the sensory organs of ears, eyes, nose, tongue and skin.[53] This casting out of strange gods occurs through the purification of senses by renouncing the pleasures of seven cardinal vices such as:- Pride, Avarice, Lust, Anger, Gluttony, Envy and Sloth. As one begins to practice the renouncement of the world of bodily senses, the soul gradually gets perfected through the gentle communications and good inspirations that comes from God. The soul that surrender to the beloved in union of love occupies all the energy pertaining to the sensory part, along with the emotions and passions of joy, hope, fear and sorrow from the first instant for the service of the Beloved.[54]

ii. Sensuality - with its inclinations

The lower part not only consists of the sense organs but also consists of the functions of the senses such as of smell, taste, touch, hearing and sight as well as the imagination and fantasy which are so close to the sensuality. These functions correspond to the sensory organs

---

51 John of the Cross, "The Ascent of Mount Carmel" in Keiran Kavanaugh, Otilio Rodriguez, (tr.), *Collected Works*, (Carmel International Publishing House, Trivandrum, Kerala, 2006) p. 76.

52 John of the Cross, A.I. ch. 15, *The Collected Works*, p. 105.

53 John of the Cross, A.I. ch. 3:1-6, *The Collected Works*, p. 76-77.

54 John of the Cross, S. C. stz. 3:18, *The Collected Works*, p. 521.

of the body. The negative appetites or the inclinations that may remain within this sensuality can cause the person to be deprived of God's Spirit and these may weary, torment, darken, defile, and weaken the soul. Hence, through a habitual denial and rejection of these appetites one must purify oneself of their influences.[55] In other words, after rejecting a sinful action, one must get healed of that sinful inclination and negative joy which comes from the effect of that sin. When the thought of God is absent, our delight in visible objects may cause sinful inclinations within us. Through the negation of these inclinations one may come closer to purity. John of the Cross compares the lower sensory part of the soul to Judea because it is weak, carnal and blind like the Judean people. Imaginations, phantasies, movements and affections of the lower part are called 'girls' as girls attract lovers by their affection and grace. So, the inclinations in this lower part strive to bring the rational and interior part into conformity with the sensory.[56] Thus, the sense organs and the functions of the sensory part of the body unless purified remains negative and if it is purified in all its inclinations it slowly helps to facilitate the journey.

1.1.2. Higher Part of the Soul[57]

By learning to leave from the world of sensory appetites or inclinations and form them to live a life that is ruled by the principles of divine love and knowledge, the journey reaches to a higher stage and the soul is able to look a bit deeper into the self and towards God with a renewed understanding. Here knowledge becomes acknowledgements[58] and the principles in life arise not merely from the sensual level but from spiritual values also.[59] This higher part consists of the rational faculties such as intellect, memory and will along with the spiritual potencies, i.e., the center of the soul or

55 John of the Cross, A.I. ch.5, *The Collected Works,* pp. 83-84.

56 John of the Cross, S C, Stz. 18:4, *The Collected Works,* p. 484.

57 John of the Cross, L F, Stz. 3:18, *The Collected Works*, p. 617.

58 Antonio Rosmini, Denis Cleary, Terence Watson (tr.), *Development of the Human Soul,* V. 2, 167.

59 Eulogio Pacho, *The Art of Reaching God According to St John of the Cross,* pp. 91-93.

conscience with divine spirit. In the higher part of the soul, mind or the interior faculties of intellect, memory and will are the faculties and they take the role of a bridle or hook in controlling and regulating the exterior senses in choosing the right and perfecting the soul by taking to the summit of the self where a soul can reach in setting its goal. Often this part functions as the internal organs of the soul. In this stage one comes to know how intellect with divine knowledge in faith can enable persons to acquire a way of life that is submissive to the divine will and how memory can annihilate or purify everything with a hope in Christ who emptied himself in order to fill us with the fullness of God and how the will can employ all its passions, appetites, operations and emotions of the soul in and towards the intended focus. Here, it reaches to a stage where one's concepts in life changes by passing through a confused stage of purgation to the right concepts.

i. Intellect[60]

In order to do the will of the other one shall know the other as perfect as he/she can and be attuned to the mind of the other as possible. When this factor is applied in the spiritual and theological level who knows whom becomes an important factor. In the case of God man relationship, the question of whose mind is to be attuned with whom also become a matter of discussion. One could naturally say here that since man's intellect got corrupted (cf. Gen 3), God gave an intellect in Jesus which is model and ideal that we can imitate perfectly. To the question "for who has known the mind of the Lord? (Rom 11:34), Jesus gives an answer in full conviction in the following way: "righteous Father, the world does not know you, but I know you".Though God's mind is hidden to us, mind of Christ that is the visible mind of God is revealed in the form of the Word of God. Hence, knowing Christ's mind through the Word of God is the perfection of knowledge (cf. Eph 2:13-14). St. Paul says that "for in him all the fullness of God was pleased to dwell" (Col 1:19). Here John gives an analysis of the knowledge that God profuse to the human intellect and the soul is able to be clothed in a new garment;

60 John of the Cross, A, II. Chs. 8-32, *The Collected Works*, pp. 125-212.

a new understanding of God with the support of a lighted candle – Christ.[61]

Intellect formed of Faith

It is a process of acquiring a way of life that enables us to surrender our intellect and knowledge in a total submission to God with all our experiences of life in faith. This way of life may be negative or positive and incomprehensible to our understanding but it is an art of learning to admit them wholly to the all surpassing knowledge of God in an eyeless faith.[62] As we mentioned before, intellect with divine knowledge is the guide in this journey. It is this intellect that is formed through faith can straighten the narrow way to the high mountain. This task can be completed only if one is able to love God in Christ by removal of obstacles related to the sensory and spiritual part of the soul.[63] In our natural way of knowing, the intellect can only grasp an object through the forms and phantasms of things perceived by the bodily senses. In this logic everything the intellect can understand, the will experience, and the imagination picture is most unlike and disproportionate to God. "Learn to be empty of all things – interiorly – and exteriorly – and you will behold that I am God" (Ps 45:11). Here, a total surrender to God is the logic of the intellect formed in faith.

ii. Memory[64]

Memory is classified by John according to the objects of the memory. They are: natural, supernatural imaginative and spiritual.

The Natural Memory includes all the natural knowledge that can be formed in the memory from the objects of the five corporal senses; hearing, sight, smell, taste, and touch.[65] The eradication of

---

61 John of the Cross, S C, stz. 1:1; stz. 37:2, *The Collected Works*, p. 416; p. 550.

62 John of the Cross, "The Dark Night", II. Ch. 21:4, *The Collected Works*, p. 378-379.

63 John of the Cross, A, II. Chs. 7-8, *Collected Works of St. John of the Cross*, pp. 121-128.

64 John of the Cross, A. III. Chs. 1-15, *The Collected Works*, pp. 213-237.

65 John of the Cross A. III. Ch. 2:4, in Keiran Kavanaugh, Otilio Rodriguez, (tr.), *St. John of the Cross, Collected Works*, p. 214.

the memory with all these forms is the primary requirement for union with God. This union cannot be wrought without a complete separation of the memory from all forms that are not God. If we turn our memory to these objects we have to meet imperfections at every step.

The Supernatural imaginative memory derives from supernatural apprehensions such as visions, revelations, locutions and sentiments. If it is a hindrance to the union with God in pure and integral hope, we have to empty itself of all that is not of God.[66] While wandering for satisfactions and answers from all these means we may stop proceeding to the centre where God awaits in His fullness.

The Spiritual memory is from spiritual knowledge. If the remembrance of this knowledge does not produce any good effect or spiritual renewal, the soul should never desire the memory of it.[67] They delicately contaminate the soul with impurity, even though the knowledge and reflection concerns God. Hence, we have to overcome this memory. When memory swallows up in things that are worthless, the soul that has hope in Christ the Crucified, will be lifted up from being absorbed in anything that is not God or God's ways.

iii. The Will[68]

The 'will' has the task of controlling the passions and desires. According to John, it also governs the memory and the understanding.[69] In the command of the Lord "you shall love the Lord your God with all your heart, and with all your soul, and with all your mind, and

66 John of the Cross, A. III. Ch. 7:1, in Keiran Kavanaugh, Otilio Rodriguez, (tr.), *St. John of the Cross, Collected Works,* p. 224; Martin Joseph Kurisumkal, *The Purification of Memory According to St. John of the Cross,* (Universidad Pontificia, Comillas Madrid, Facultad DeTeologia Instituto De Espiritualidad, 2011) pp. 63-64.

67 John of the Cross, A. III. Ch. 14:1-2, in Keiran Kavanaugh, Otilio Rodriguez, (tr.), *St. John of the Cross, Collected Works*, pp. 234-235.

68 John of the Cross, A. III. Ch. 16-45, in Keiran Kavanaugh, Otilio Rodriguez, (tr.), *The Collected Works of St. John of the Cross*, pp. 237-292.

69 Norbert Cummins, *An Introduction to St. John of the Cross,* (Darlington Carmel, [Private circulation only]) p. 51.

with all your strength" (Mt. 22:37) man is invited to employ all the faculties, passions, appetites, operations, and emotions of his soul in God and towards God. From these faculties, passions and appetites are the strength of the soul and the will should act upon their stimuli according to the rational understanding and principles formed from the knowledge.[70]

a) Knowledge with a New Understanding of God[71]

When the will directs passions, and appetites toward God, the soul preserves its strength for God and comes to love Him with all its might. In the beginning when the flame of love is not so bright the person suffers great deprivation and afflictions in the spirit even affects the senses with extreme oppression. Here, instead of the flame of love the flame of purgatory seems to be in the heights and the soul feels that: God has changed his mind and He is cruel towards me.[72] To explain these wounded feelings of soul towards God, John of the Cross quotes from the book of Lamentations:

> I am one who has seen affliction under the rod of God's wrath; he has driven and brought me into darkness without any light; against me alone he turns his hand, again and again, all day long. He has made my flesh and my skin waste away, and broken my bones; he has besieged and enveloped me with bitterness and tribulation; he has made me sit in darkness like the dead of long ago. He has walled me about so that I cannot escape; he has put heavy chains on me; though I call and cry for help, he shuts out my prayer; he has blocked my ways with hewn stones, he has made my paths crooked (Lam 3:1-9).

---

70 E.W. Trueman Dicken, *The Crucible of Love, A Study of the Mysticism of St. Teresa of Jesus and St. John of the Cross*, (Sheed and Ward, New York, 1963) p. 333.

71 John of the Cross, A. I. Ch. 5:7, in Keiran Kavanaugh, Otilio Rodriguez, (tr.), *Collected Works*, p. 83.

72 John of the Cross, L. F. 1:21-22 in Keiran Kavanaugh, Otilio Rodriguez, (tr.), *Collected Works*, p. 587.

The feeling of this intense suffering and purgation leads or misguides the person to understand God in a totally different way. One can find many examples from the scripture itself. Some of the reflections are as follows:

a) God is a selfish and unjust one acquiring the best of everything for Himself alone (Gen 3:22; Job 10:13);
b) God a strict observer like mere man (Gen 3: 24; Job 7:12, 20; 10:5-6);
c) God a Ruler and a wrong Judge like a Lion (Gen 3:8; Job 10:16; Hos 13:7);
d) God who snatches away like an eagle and sitting in the throne of heaven (Job 16:19; 39:28-29);
e) God who left me out to work like an ox (Gen 3:17; Job 7:1).

In explaining the purgative feeling of the soul John of the Cross presents the simile from the Book of Tobit where Tobias burning the fish's heart and liver to drive out every kind of demon or evil spirit which afflicts the person. Similarly, at the stage of transformation all the infirmities are brought to light and the souls begin to see everything with right perceptions and notions. It is a slow and gradual process passing through the contraries of understandings. Here there is conflict of contraries against the contraries: the awfully perfect virtues and properties of God, stand against the enormously imperfect habits and properties of the soul. God here transforms the purgative flame by softening, pacifying and clarifying every experiences of life through grace in the soul.[73] Consequently, the souls turn towards God with a new understanding.

b) Will with Bridled Passions

In this John of the Cross refers four feelings or passions in his book the Ascend of the Mount Carmel. Those feelings are joy, hope, sorrow, and fear.[74] When these passions are unbridled, they are the source of all the vices and imperfections and when they are in order

73 John of the Cross, L. F. 1:23, in Keiran Kavanaugh, Otilio Rodriguez, (tr.), *St. John of the Cross, Collected Works,* p. 588.

74 John of the Cross, A. III. Ch. 16:2, *Collected Works,* p. 237.

and composed they give rise to all the virtues.[75] Here at this stage, the soul learns to bridle and form these passions positively towards pure inclinations through charity. A soul in its journey gains nothing, if it neglects the purification of the will through charity.[76]

1.1.3. The Centre of the Soul

In his book the Living Flame of Love, John of the Cross says that the soul's centre is God. When the soul with its full capacity of being and the strength of its operation and inclination, it attains its final and deepest centre who is God; it will know, love and enjoy God with all its might.[77] This is the deepest and most intimate part of one's being of the soul. Just as Prophet Ezekiel speaks of the most holy place as the place of 'my Throne and Top of the Mountain'; in his spiritual canticle John of the Cross speaks of this Mountain where the soul finds its most beautiful state for the union, knowledge and wisdom of God.[78]

The highest part of the soul or the centre of the soul is recognized here as the deepest centre of one's soul where one knows, loves and enjoys God with all its might. This is the sanctuary of our soul or the mountain top. When one reaches this stage the Spirit of God takes the control of man who is built upon the divine conscience and the devil cannot know how mysteriously God works in such souls who are submissive to God. Hence, this part will give the picture of a stage where one reaches with no other considerations except the divine will.

To reach this state one need a withdrawal of all things interesting to the soul from the lower sensory portion and higher rational part comprising the entire compound of man's faculties and senses which is called 'hill'. Here the hill must be free from any particular knowledge, affection or other considerations in any of the spiritual faculties like intellect, memory and will or other natural operations in any of the bodily senses and faculties either in interior or exterior.

75 John of the Cross, S. C. Chs. 20; 21:9-15, *Collected Works*, pp. 491-494.

76 John of the Cross, A. III. Ch.16:1, *Collected Works,* p. 237.

77 John of the Cross, L. F. 1: 13, *Collected Works,* p. 583.

78 John of the Cross, S. C. stz. 36:6, *Collected Works,* p. 547.

Only the will appears attending to the Beloved with a total surrender of self.[79]

1.2. Steps or Ladder According to St. John of the Cross

John analyses how a soul in sojourn passes through faith with steps and articles of a life that is hazardous. Though everything in life seems to be dark, the soul with faith will pass its entire stairs. And also explains how this ladder becomes secret as the hidden manna. It also gives an explanation of various degrees of love and holiness through passing each levels or steps. The steps here are structured to express or present an inward journey from sensory world to the interior self. These steps will enable persons to overcome the appetites and passions of the lower part or sensory level, and perfect the interior senses with faith by self - forgetfulness and detaching the intellect, memory and will from everything that are contrary to the love of God. John also speaks of Ladder or steps as undisclosed and disguised; ('by the secret ladder, disguised').[80] It is secret because all the stairs or articles of faith are secret and hidden from both the senses and intellect. As a consequence, for the soul everything in life seems to be dark. But, the senses and intellect can travel without light and goes beyond every natural and rational boundaries to climb the divine ladder of faith that 'penetrates even to the heights of God.'[81]

The ladder is secret because of the wisdom that comes through the contemplation and the effects it produces in the soul is secret. Language of God is ineffable because it transcends everything sensory and it is very spiritual and intimate to the soul. It immediately silences the entire ability and it is the harmonious composite of the exterior and interior senses. Still the ladder is secret because it hides the soul within itself. The soul is conscious of being more hidden as it is elevated above every temporal creatures. The way to God is hidden and secret to the sensory part and the traces and footsteps

79 John of the Cross, S. C. stz. 16:10, in Keiran Kavanaugh, Otilio Rodriguez, (tr.), *St. John of the Cross, Collected Works*, p. 587.

80 John of the Cross, A. II. Ch. 1:1, *Collected Works*, p. 105.

81 John of the Cross, A. II. Ch. 1:1, *Collected Works,* p. 105.

God leaves in those whom He desires to bring to Himself through union with His wisdom are unrecognizable.[82]

The secret wisdom is a "ladder" because, by the secret contemplation, the soul ascends in order to plunder, know, and possess the goods and treasures of heaven. This secret wisdom is a ladder because as the same steps of a ladder are used for both ascent and descent, the same communications this secret contemplation produces in the soul worship of God and humiliation within itself.[83]

The degree of love and holiness that a soul possesses as it grows in the knowledge of God is represented as steps or ladder for John. The soul may not be able to possess it at a stretch or in one day, in a month or even within a year. After the gentle touch that soul receives in the initial stage, the journey it begins will be a gradual process of growth and progression. In this journey the soul advances in God from its lower level to the highest with an intensity that each soul is capable to receive. So, it is necessary to know the depth and development of the degree of holiness in a person.

1.2.1. Degree of Holiness - of The Lower Part of The Soul[84] - 7 Steps

As the journey gradually moves on, the soul gets an advanced form, a spiritual mantle of seven cardinal sins which John explains in his book "The Dark Night" as seven steps one need to climb in order to reach the base level of holiness.[85] Without mounting the base steps which are the capital vices, no one can grow to and live a life of grace. Only one who has faith will be able to climb these steps and enter into this dark night of faith. These capital vices are the imperfections of the beginners who are in their inner journey but hidden in their souls with a spiritual mantle. The soul before entering into the

82 John of the Cross, D. N. II. Ch. 17:1-8, in Keiran Kavanaugh, Otilio Rodriguez, (tr.), *St. John of the Cross, Collected* Works, pp. 368-371.

83 John of the Cross, D. N. II. Ch. 18, in Keiran Kavanaugh, Otilio Rodriguez, (tr.), *St. John of the Cross, Collected Works*, p. 371.

84 John of the Cross, D. N. I. Ch. 2-7, in Keiran Kavanaugh, Otilio Rodriguez, (tr.), *St. John of the Cross, Collected Works*, pp. 299-310.

85 John of the Cross, D. N., I. Ch. 2-7, in Keiran Kavanaugh, Otilio Rodriguez, (tr.), *St. John of the Cross, Collected Works*, pp. 299-310.

passive night of the senses is satisfied with itself because its 'penances are pleasures' and 'its fasts, happiness'. As a result, the soul cultivates within the 'spiritual mantle', the seven capital vices: - Pride, Avarice, Lust, Anger, Gluttony, Envy and Sloth. By climbing these seven steps the soul will be able to overcome the appetites and passions of the lower part of the soul.[86]

To unite oneself in grace with God, this one degree of love or practice of holiness in the lower part alone is sufficient.[87] To remain in this grace and degree of love, one needs to climb the steps of faith by overcoming the seven cardinal sins first in its own literal sense. The soul begins the journey only after an encounter with God and a decision to renounce its evil ways which previously lived. Without passing these steps in both exteriorly by removal of their experience from the sensory organs and spiritually by overcoming their residue in the further stage of growth, no one can reach the other end of holiness passing through the second level with a deeper commitment in loving God and knowing oneself. This is a glance into the degree of love the soul begins to enter to love God in its own perfection.[88]

1.2.2. Degree of Holiness - of the Higher Part of the Soul - 8 Steps

After having climbed up the seven steps from the lower part of the soul by annihilating seven cardinal vices, the soul is ready to depart for a journey in *faith* by perfecting the *intellect.* It is only by forming an intellect with faith that germinates divine knowledge one can withstand the windy areas of life. John proposes mainly eight steps for our knowledge to choose in order to advance in this. The following are the main steps:

1. Not to the easiest, but to the most difficult
2. Not to the delightful, but to the most distasteful

86 John of the Cross, D. N. I. Ch. 2-7, in Keiran Kavanaugh, Otilio Rodriguez, (tr.), *St. John of the Cross, Collected Works,* pp. 299-310.

87 John of the Cross, L. F. stz. I. Ch. 1:13, in Keiran Kavanaugh, Otilio Rodriguez, (tr.), *St. John of the Cross, Collected Works,* p. 583.

88 John of the Cross, L. F. stz. I. Ch. 1:13, in Keiran Kavanaugh, Otilio Rodriguez, (tr.), *St. John of the Cross, Collected Works,* p. 584.

3. Not to the most gratifying, but to the less pleasant
4. Not to what means rest for you, but to hard work
5. Not to the consoling, but to the un-consoling
6. Not to the most, but to the least
7. Not to the highest and most precious, but to the lowest and most despised
8. Not to wanting something, but to wanting nothing.

After having exercised in the above said eight steps for perfecting the intellect, again in *hope* the soul is set for a further advancing by perfecting the *memory*. John says that the spiritual departure refers two ways of going after God. In this the first one consists of a withdrawal from all things, effected through a disdain for them and the second, in going out from oneself through self – forgetfulness which is achieved by the love of God.[89] In perfecting the memory, the following steps are made use of:

1. To reach satisfaction in all, desire its possession in nothing.
2. To come to possess all, desire the possession of nothing.
3. To arrive at being all, desire to be nothing.
4. To come to the knowledge of all, desire the knowledge of nothing.
5. To come to the pleasure you have not, you must go by a way in which you enjoy not.
6. To come to the knowledge you have not, you must go by a way in which you know not.
7. To come to the possession you have not, you must go by a way in which you possess not.
8. To come to be what you are not, you must to go by a way in which you are not.

At this level the soul is set for a further advancing in *charity* by perfecting the *will*. As described above here also there are eight steps in the formation of it. Here the will united with the divine love, no longer loves in a lowly manner with its natural strength, but loves with the strength and purity of the Holy Spirit. Here in

89 John of the Cross, S. C. stz. 1:20, in Keiran Kavanaugh, Otilio Rodriguez, (tr.), *St. John of the Cross, Collected Works*, p. 423.

the soul's journey the active and passive grace is fused in one step of charity. For the perfection of the will in charity the following steps are observed:

1. Soul receives the loving light and wisdom that in the beginning purges and prepares it.
2. Recognizing and accepting that the suffering does not derive from this wisdom but from the soul's own weakness and imperfection (Ezek. 39:23).
3. The soul infers the manner in which souls suffer in purgatory. Accepts the suffering here on earth with the recognition that when the imperfections are gone, the soul's suffering terminates, and joy remains.[90]
4. The soul purged and purified by the fire of love, is further enkindled in love and the good effects are revealed.
5. The soul after this alleviation suffers again, more intensely and inwardly than before and by that, penetrates more deeply into the wood and its action becomes stronger and more vehement, preparing the innermost part in order to gain possession of it.
6. The soul discovers the reason; for at this time it is conscious of nothing but its own bitterness. The soul's joy will be more interior because of the more intimate purification.
7. The soul deduce that the purification is soon to return, even though the soul's joy is ample during these intervals, there is a feeling, that some root remains. When the soul does have this feeling, the purification soon returns.
8. Finally, more inward part still to be eliminated and illumined, the purification returns to attack more interiorly. Once again the soul thinks all its good has come to an end and that its blessings are over. Placed in these more interior sufferings, it is blinded as to all exterior good.[91]

---

90 John of the Cross, L .F, stz. 1:24, in Keiran Kavanaugh, Otilio Rodriguez, (tr.), *St. John of the Cross, Collected Works,* p. 589.

91 John of the Cross, D. N. II. Ch. 10 in Keiran Kavanaugh, Otilio Rodriguez, (tr.), *St. John of the Cross, Collected Works,* p. 350.

1.2.3. Degree of Holiness - of The Centre of The Soul[92] - 10 Steps

John of the Cross in his book 'The Dark night' teaches the 10 steps of mystical ladder that a soul passes while climbing the mountain of perfection and union with God in perfect love.

i. The love that makes the soul sick

As a sick person changes colour and loses his appetite for all foods, in this step of love the soul changes the colour of its past life and loses its appetite for all things, especially the things of the world.

ii. Searching God unceasingly

It resembles the bride who is searching the bridegroom, after asking the guards for the bridegroom immediately passed by and left them behind (Song 3:3-4). When eating, sleeping, keeping vigil or doing anything else, it centres all its care on the Beloved.

iii. Promptness in performance of works

Because of his intense love of God, a person at this stage feels deep sorrow and pain even in the slight offences he does for God. The soul thinks the great works it does for the Beloved are small; its many works, few; the long time spent in His service, short. In this third step the soul is far removed from vainglory, presumption, and the condemnation of others.

The person thinks inwardly that he is really worse than all others. The reason for this effect is that love is teaching him what God deserves.

iv. A habitual yet, un-wearisome suffering

The spirit possesses so much energy on this step that it brings the flesh under control and takes little account of it. The soul in no way seeks consolation or satisfaction either in God or in anything else; neither does it desire or ask favours of God, for it is clearly aware that it has already received many from Him. This degree of love is a

92 John of the Cross, D. N. II. Ch. 19-20, in Keiran Kavanaugh, Otilio Rodriguez, (tr.), *St. John of the Cross, Collected Works*, pp. 373-378.

very elevated step as the soul at this stage pursues God in the spirit of suffering for His sake.

v. An impatient desire and longing for God

In this step the desire of the lover to apprehend and to unit with the Beloved is so ardent that any delay, no matter how slight, is long, annoying, and tiresome. The soul is ever - believing that it is finding its Beloved; and when it sees its desire frustrated, which is at almost every step, it faints in its longing. In this step, the lover must either see its love or die. In this step of hunger, the soul so feeds on love, for its hunger is its satisfaction.

vi. Runs swiftly to God

The sixth step makes the soul run swiftly toward God in an experience of God's touch. By hope it runs without fainting. Love invigorates it to fly swiftly. The soul's charity is now highly increased and almost completely purified. Therefore, the soul is soon brought from the sixth step to the seventh step.

vii. An Ardent boldness

At this stage love neither profits by the judgment to wait nor makes use of the counsel to retreat, neither can it be restricted through shame. The favour God now gives it imparts with an ardent daring. The souls in this step obtain from God with pleasure what they ask of Him. It is illicit for the soul to become daring if it does not perceive the divine favour held out toward it, or it may fall down from the steps already climbed. On this step it must always conserve humility. Because of the unrestricted hand and boldness God gives on this seventh step, the soul climbs the eighth step.

viii. Laying hold of the beloved

Although the soul satisfies its desire on this step of union, it does not do so continually. Some manage to get to it, but soon turn back and leave it. If one remains on this step, a certain glory would be possessed in this life; so, the soul rests on it for only a short period of time. Referring to Daniel (Dan 10:11) John speaks that, because the prophet Daniel was a man of desires, God ordered him to stay on this step.

ix. Burning gently with love

The ninth step of love causes the soul to burn gently. It is the step of the perfect who burns gently in God. The Holy Spirit produces his gentle and delightful ardour by reason of the perfect soul's union with God. The saint says that the goods and riches of God a man enjoys on this step are numerous and an attempt to record it will be an imperfect action.

x. Assimilating the soul to God completely

In the tenth and last step of this secret ladder of love assimilates the soul to God completely because of the clear vision of God which a person possesses as soon as he reaches it. It is the actualization of what is said in John 16:23 "on that day you will ask nothing of me". On this last step of clear vision at the top of the ladder, where God rests, nothing is hidden from the soul because of its total assimilation. However, by means of this secret love, the soul departs from itself and all things and ascends to God. For love is like fire which always rises upwards as though longing to be engulfed in its centre. In short, love is the guide in this Mystical ladder.

1.3. Breeze and Winds for John of the Cross

When the Hebrew Scriptures refer to the winds from four sides (east, west, north and south) are usually mentioned with some latitude of meaning and are distinctly recognised. Wind, for the Israelites, was divine energy in the nature. Looking at the type, nature, functions of the wind, we can recognize various forms of wind or recognize its direction. There are winds in different forms, measure or weight, speed and with specific function.[93] In the Book of Genesis one can observe that God comes in the Evening Breeze: Making an awareness of one's own nakedness (cf. Gen 3:8). Gentle Breeze/Evening Breeze

93 Smith J., Acworth A., Hemer C. J "Wind", *The Illustrated Bible Dictionary*, Part 3, (ed.) Parable-Zuzim, Mary Gladstone (et.al), (InterVarsity Press, Tyndale House Publishers, UK, 1980) p. 1647.

can stand for a kind of indication, awareness, presence, healing, comforting, and smoothening etc.

For John, breeze stands for the touch and the whistling or sound. So, when divine love is paralleled to breeze, it communicates knowledge and a feeling of delight. The feel of the breeze delights the sense of touch which represents the attributes of the Beloved. Its whistling represents the sense of hearing which can be the knowledge of these attributes experienced in the intellect.[94] In the Spiritual Canticle one reads "Be still, deadening north wind;"[95] It is apt to call deadening, because according to the Book of Proverbs the north wind 'produces rain, and a backbiting tongue, angry looks' (Prov 25: 23). This can be the evil that happens in our rational faculties or in intellect. John narrates that, the north wind is very cold, it dries up and withers the flowers and plants, or at least striking them makes shrink and close. The spiritual dryness and affective absence of the Beloved produces this same effect in the soul by extinguishing the satisfaction, delight, and fragrance of the virtues she was enjoying, she calls it a 'deadening north wind'.

In the Spiritual Canticle we read: "South wind come, you that awakens love."[96] Referring to the south wind in the book Job we read, "you whose garments are hot when the earth is still because of the south wind (Job 37:17)". For John, south wind is a delightful breeze; it causes rain, makes the herbs and plants germinate opens the flowers and scatters their fragrance. Its effects are the opposite of those of the north wind. The soul, by this breeze refers to the Holy Spirit, who awakens love.[97]

Warm winds also blow from the South.[98] Just as the south wind warms up everything, the memory makes everything still and allows the person to look back or to live in the past instead of travelling

---

94 John of the Cross, S. C. stz. 14, 15:12-15, in Keiran Kavanaugh, Otilio Rodriguez, (tr.), *St. John of the Cross, Collected Works,* pp. 467-469.

95 John of the Cross, S. C. stz. 17:3, *Collected Works,* p. 479.

96 John of the Cross, S. C stz. 17:4, *Collected Works*, p. 480.

97 John of the Cross, S. C. stz. 17:4, *Collected Works* , p. 480.

98 Smith J., Acworth A., Hemer C. J "Wind", *The Illustrated Bible Dictionary,* Part 3, (ed.) Parable-Zuzim, Mary Gladstone (et.al), (InterVarsity Press, Tyndale House Publishers, UK, 1980) p. 1647.

to the right reason, God Himself. With a wounded memory and negative mind, no one can have a right understanding of God or man.

1.3.1. Three Theological Virtues As Offerings[99]

John speaks on the importance of growing in theological virtues in this process of integral growth. In the journey of oneself and others in progression towards God the soul is advised to take three forms of precautions or means which are: faith, hope and charity that support the souls from being defeated by the three enemies such as world, flesh and devil that one may constantly encounter on the way in various forms and means. For him the theological virtues faith hope and charity fight against the three fundamental enemies ever seen in the created earth. Actually, these virtues protect from powers that would hinder us from encountering God. Each theological virtue is attributed to each human faculties respectively: faith to the intellect, hope to the faculty of memory and charity to the faculty of will.[100]

i. Intellect and Faith

More than all other virtues, faith gives a strong protection to the soul against the devil. The white tunic of faith protects the intellect from being hindered by the enemy and an intellect formed of faith is a strong weapon for the simple and ignorant one's to fight against the enemy, devil. Quoting the psalmist, John emphasises the importance of the word of God in rooting and protecting oneself with faith.[101] Following these words of the psalmist we understand that it is a commitment and full submission of one's intellect and will to God who reveals Himself through His Word. A life bound with the Word of God becomes an encounter with the person Jesus Christ, whom

99 John of the Cross, D. N. II. Ch. 21, *Collected Works*, pp. 378-381.

100 John of the Cross, A. II. Ch. 6, in Keiran Kavanaugh, Otilio Rodriguez, (tr.), *St. John of the Cross, Collected Works*, pp. 119-120; Jacob Palliparambil, "Theological life: a Programme for Spiritual Life", in *St. John of the Cross, Studies on his Life, Doctrine and Time*, Justine Panakal, (ed.), Jyothir Dhara Publications, Kalamassery, 1991) p. 65.

101 John of the Cross, D. N. II. Ch. 21, Collected Works, pp. 379.

we entrust our whole life.[102] The power and grace that is infused into us through our life in Christ is unfolded in faith again as Signs. This faith enables one to present his life as an offering to God and cultivate a way of life that encounter Christ who emptied Himself to meet our every need.

ii. Memory and Hope

When John distinguishes 'faith' with the white tunic, he uses the image of the green coloured garment for 'hope' to differentiate it with the first. The virtue of hope is the proper instrument through which the soul may guard and free oneself from the second enemy, the world. This greenness of living hope in God and eternal life enable souls to look at the things of the world as truly dry, withered, dead, and worthless. Through this hope the soul obtains from God all that it hopes to receive from Him.[103] In the disguise of the green costume of hope one acquires the willingness to enter into the dark and secret night by emptying of all possessions, support and cares of the world, this in turn is one's voluntary entering into a process of healing the memory by the support of the guidance and light from Him, Christ and His Spirit. By this voluntary process, memory is not only healed but enabled to travel ahead to a supernatural life by conquering the natural self by giving all the hopes and memories of oneself as a constant offering to Christ.

iii. Will and Love

As a continuation of what is said above and as the finishing touch and perfection of this disguise the soul puts on a third colour, over the white and green, a precious red garment. This colour denotes charity, the third virtue, that not only adds elegance to the other two but so elevates the soul as to place it near God. Charity makes the soul so beautiful and pleasing to God. With this dress of charity, which increases love for the Beloved, the soul receives protection and concealment from the flesh, its third enemy. For where there is true

---

102 Benedict XVI, Verbum Domini, (Post Synodal Apostolic Exhortation on the Word of God in the Life and Mission of the Church, Sept 30, 2010), "Carmel International Publishing House, Trivandrum 2011, pp. 49-50.

103 John of the Cross, D. N. II. Ch. 21:6, *Collected Works*, pp. 379.

love of God, love of self and of one's own things finds no entry. Not only does charity protect the soul, but it even makes the other virtues genuine, strengthens and invigorates them in order to fortify the soul, and bestows on them loveliness and charm so as to please the Beloved thereby. For without charity no virtue is pleasing to God. The soul is clothed in this red costume when, as explained in the first stanza of "The Ascend of Mount Carmel", it departs in the dark night from itself and from all creatures, passionate with love's urgent longings,[104] and advances by the secret ladder of contemplation to perfect union with God Who is its beloved salvation. The essence of reaching union with God consists in purging the will of its appetites and feelings. There is no perfect charity without a life of constant sacrifice. Hence, a will with love is a life of offering. In order to share love, the soul must first of all fill with the Beloved's own love. This is the love of Christ which He fills in the soul. Though such supernatural experiences are not continuous or constant in this life, as gratitude, presenting one's life as an offering of love is a constant process.[105]

1.3.2. Love of Christ at the Inmost Centre

For John, Christ is the reason of his love, centre of his focus, Christ is the rock, He is the deepest centre in seeking wisdom, and He himself is the gate to enter into it. The mysteries of Christ and the attributes, mysteries, judgments, and virtues of God in Christ are symbolized and expressed in many ways and forms throughout his writings just like his example of pomegranates with many little seeds within the circular shell.[106] The sublime, exalted and deep mysteries of God's wisdom in Christ are called as high caverns because of the height of the sublime mysteries. Caverns are deep and have many recesses, so each of the mysteries in Christ is singularly deep in wisdom. Christ for him is like an abundant mine with many recesses of treasures. So even though the soul dive deep in to the inner most recesses they

---

104 John of the Cross, A. I. Ch. 1, in Keiran Kavanaugh, Otilio Rodriguez, (tr.), *St. John of the Cross, Collected Works,* p. 73.

105 John of the Cross, S. C. stz. 26:11, *Collected Works,* p. 513.

106 John of the Cross, S. C. stz. 37:7, Collected Works, p. 552.

never reach the end or bottom, but everywhere find new traces with new riches.[107]

i. Christ's Love Never Oppresses

According to John, before the soul reaches its centre, the life it experiences is with strong appetites in the exterior senses, sharp trials in the intellect, severe dryness and distress in the will and burdensome knowledge of one's own miseries in the memory. The soul finds no relief in anything, no consolation, nor even able to raise heart to God because it is so oppressed by this flame. This flame in the beginning provides the sight to see the clear picture of one. But, at this stage the will and passions were not so united with God to consider the fulfilment of God's will as its glory. But, when the soul reaches at the centre at the stage of union, the soul finds its centre in God and following the narrow way of Christ becomes a glory for the soul. The sufferings will be no more oppressive.[108] God's will be identified with the will of the soul. At this stage one is able to confess in gentleness to God at every moment that:

> "You are the divine light of my intellect by which I can look at you,
> You are the strength of my will and have ceased making me faint in my weakness,
> You are no longer heavy and constraint to the substance of my soul, but glory, delight and amplitude."[109]

ii. Life in the Holy Spirit: Death to the Past and Alive in God

According to John, God's love produces four goods in the soul. 1) It cleanses, 2) Endows with grace, 3) Enriches, 4) Illumines. In this state of the soul, God no longer remembers its former malice and sin. She becomes very agreeable to Him. Once He has blotted out this sin and malice, He no longer reproaches her for it, nor fails to impart

---

107 John of the Cross, S. C. stz. 36, 37, in Keiran Kavanaugh, Otilio Rodriguez, (tr.), *St. John of the Cross, Collected Works,* pp. 545-552.

108 John of the Cross, L. F. stz. 1:18, *Collected Works*, p. 586.

109 John of the Cross, L. F. stz. 1:26, *Collected Works*, p. 589.

more favours, since He never judges a thing twice.[110] It is "forgetting what lies behind and straining forward to what lies ahead" (Phil 3: 13).The one who is in journey should hold fast the grace and Spirit of Christ that he has attained (Phil 3:16). After this transformation, the soul possesses character of a 'dove' i.e. simple, meek, without gall, bright and with loving eyes. It is a change in the attitude and approach that one possesses towards God, oneself and others in the daily realities of life. The soul gets this form because this is what she assimilates from her God.[111]

1.3.2.1. The Cross as Tree of Life and Gate to Enter into the River of Wisdom

For John of the Cross, one who is able to stand beneath the Cross of Christ and look ahead can only restore his genuine nature that was lost and can draw good from evil so wisely and beautifully.[112] For John of the Cross, one who wish to gain wisdom needs to join with Christ's mind and make it pass through the gate of Cross in order to get purified of its natural passions, appetites, emotions, distress etc., and to be judged and evaluated with the measuring reed and cord, Christ the Crucified.[113] In Christ there are deep mysteries of God's wisdom. A life evaluated with the measuring reed and cord, Christ the Crucified will be a transformed river of wisdom that flows everywhere in peace (cf. Col 1:20).

1.3.2.2 Water Sides and River of Wisdom

For John of the Cross the mortifications, penances and spiritual exercises by which the soul practices the active and contemplative life together are similar to watersides which are low. But, virtuous life represents the high mountain because of the difficulty and labour one undergoes in climbing them.[114] In comparing the nature of river and the soul he characterizes the river with its three properties: First,

110 John of the Cross, S. C. stz. 33:1, *Collected Works*, p. 537.

111 John of the Cross, S. C, stz. 34:3, in Keiran Kavanaugh, Otilio Rodriguez, (tr.), *St. John of the Cross, Collected Works*, p. 541.

112 John of the Cross, S. C. stz. 23:3-6, *Collected Works,* p. 500.

113 John of the Cross, S. C. stz. 36:13, *Collected Works,* p. 549.

114 John of the Cross, S. C. stz. 3:4, *Collected Works*, p. 429.

the river surrounds and engulfs everything it encounter: in the case of the soul it feels here that all the actions and passions in which she was formerly occupied are drowned therein. Although it is with tremendous force, this is not a torment to her, because the river is river of peace. Second, the river fills up all the low and empty places on its way. In the case of the soul it experiences the filling of divine water in the low and the voids places of her humility and appetites. Third, it is so loud that they muffle and surpass every other sound. In the case of the condition of the soul this sound exceeds all other sounds of the world and so it does not contain any physical sound or its discomfort and disturbances. But, the Spirit of God will be over the chaos of this water. And it clothes the soul with grandeur, strength, power, delight and glory.[115] Hence, the river and water become the rivers of wisdom and knowledge.

It is necessary that in a journey one should have a focussing point. A Journey that is focussed at with a supportive map, will find its ultimate end with more satisfaction, accuracy and fastness. To know the right way, end, and purpose of the journey, one shouldn't focus on oneself but on the guide. If we take the above said example and apply it in our spiritual journey, the more we look at ourselves we are prone to fail but the more we guise at Christ we become perfected at every step. In Christ, there is a perfect map to eternity, and He is our best companion to take us well dressed in holiness to our Father's house. Being attuned to Christ, we possess a transmuting grace which becomes a constitutive factor in transforming us into a new creation and a living temple and abode of God. In order to perfect the human nature, an ideal self is given in Christ. And Christ becomes the way by accepting all the trials and tribulations. The suffering of Christ as a token of love especially on the cross is the motive force for the one who is aspiring for this transformation and also prevents us from being discouraged. Christ the truth refers that he is the true grace that liberates, save, strengthen and glorifies us. By presenting Christ as life one conform his will to the will of Christ and there forms only one life as God has adorned him with fullness of life.

115 John of the Cross, S. C. stz. 14, 15:25-27, *Collected Works,* pp. 472-473.

For John, possessing Christ meant possessing God and the whole creation with Him. He firmly believed that for a person who journey towards God, everything he desires is gifted in Christ.[116] For him, the attentiveness to faith is the wisdom of God in total way; that is, Son of God who is communicated to the soul in faith.[117] Now it is important to think on the subject matter Jesus the way truth and Life.

i. The Way: As it is said, "Behind every understanding of the faith lies a *way of* following Jesus."[118] For John, faith is an aptitude by which one live. It is certain as the word of God but obscure as it may not deliver proof while delivering truth.[119] The way here means the purity of faith[120] which enables persons to blind their intellect from everything that can understand, the will experience, and the imagination picture in our knowledge and attainment of God. According to John, one should blind all the knowledge grasped by the intellect through exterior or interior senses if he is attached to it or does not advance with the support of faith. Faith affirms and brings certitude to the intellect though it blinds or darkens our intellect as the brightest light in God is complete darkness to our intellect.[121] But, a union of the will with Christ[122] robed in the whiteness of

---

116 Jordan Regis, "Jesus Christ in the Writings of John of the Cross", in *Carmelite Studies, John of the Cross: Conferences and Essays by Members of The Institute of Carmelite Studies and others*, Payne Steven (ed.), (ICS Publications, Washington, D.C. 1992) p. 98.

117 Mathew Iain, The Impact of God; Soundings from St. John of the Cross, (Hodder & Stoughton Ltd., London, 2010) p. 103; John of the Cross, A. II. Ch. 29:6, in Keiran Kavanaugh, Otilio Rodriguez, (tr.), *St. John of the Cross, Collected Works*, p. 205.

118 Gustavo Gutierrez, "The Theology of Liberation" in F. Fernando Segovia (ed.), *Towards a New Heaven and a New Earth*, (Orbis Books, Mary knoll, New York 2003), p. 297.

119 Mathew Iain, *The Impact of God; Soundings from St. John of the Cross*, (Hodder & Stoughton Ltd., London, 2010), p. 103.

120 John of the Cross, A. II. Ch. 8:1-3, in Keiran Kavanaugh, Otilio Rodriguez, (tr.), *St. John of the Cross, Collected Works*, p. 126.

121 John of the Cross, A. II. Ch. 8:6, in Keiran Kavanaugh, Otilio Rodriguez, (tr.), *St. John of the Cross, Collected Works*, p. 128.

122 Mt. 12:30, John of the Cross, A. I. Ch. 11:5, *Collected Works*, p. 98.

pure faith[123] alone is a secret ladder or path[124] in our sojourn. The gate or way through which we enter into the grove of the wisdom is the cross of Christ.[125] All the trials and tribulations in our journey to the truth which prevent us from being discouraged is the love of Christ on the Cross[126] because he is the way. Truly this way is hard and narrow yet taking us to the high mountains, green meadows and fresh valleys. According to John, Christ alone is our light and guide. "With no other light or guide; than the one that burned in my heart."[127] Here, John is speaking of Christ who leads and guides; the one who is burning in his heart. This burning in the heart with the transformative love is the force that moves one on this way.

ii. The Truth: For St. John, life is a journey towards truth. This truth is the knowledge of Christ, in whom God has emptied Himself. Here the living flame of love from God is now gentle, not oppressive because the soul has seen with his/her eyes the God in Jesus, who has despised Himself for the sake of the soul.[128] He is the true grace in liberating, saving, strengthening and glorifying us. In Christ there is answer for everything. Over the white tunic of faith John invites us to put a green coat of hope which assures us that the risen Lord is living and working with us.[129] Even if everything seems dark or wrong, Christ who conquered the world can transform our life as he is "full of grace and truth."[130] Following Christ in conformity with His will, in the simplicity of life is abiding in his truth.[131] Jesus the

---

123 Susan Muto, *John of the Cross for Today: The Dark Night* (Ave Maria Publications, Indiana, 1994) p. 275.

124 John of the Cross, A. II. Ch 1:1, *Collected Works,* p. 107.

125 John of the Cross, S. C, stz. 36:13, *Collected Works*, p. 549.

126 John of the Cross, A. II. Ch. 7:6-7, *Collected Works*, p. 123; Jordan Regis, "Jesus Christ in the Writings of John of the Cross", in *Carmelite Studies, John of the Cross: Conferences and Essays by Members of the Institute of Carmelite Studies and others*, p. 104.

127 John of the Cross, D. N. II. Ch. 25, *Collected Works,* pp. 388-389.

128 Mathew Iain, The Impact of God; Soundings from St. John of the Cross, pp. 62-63.

129 John of the Cross, D. N. II. Ch. 21, Collected Works, p. 379.

130 C.C.C. "Life in Christ", #.2466, p. 651.

131 C.C.C. "Life in Christ", pp. 651-652.

truth will sanctify us from all clutches of evil inclinations and will set us free with an integral self. Hope is the virtue that detaches us from setting our hearts on things that are perishable[132] and attach our life with Christ who is truth now and for ever. God has revealed the truth in Christ who is the word that was made flesh.[133]

iii. The Life: St. John of the Cross gives emphasis on the life by saying that it is a gift we received from God in Christ. For this he is inspired from the words of John who said in his Gospel "All things were made through him, and without him was not anything made that was made" (Jn 1:3).[134] In "The Spiritual Canticle" John says that only true love brings life to the soul.[135] Life we receive as a gift of God but it is transmitted through the selfless love of Christ. Our souls are alive in God through Christ. The outcome of all the hardships one passes through in the journey is to transform one's natural life into the divine life of Christ. In this process of union, one conforms his will to the will of Christ in perfect love and as a consequence, there is only one life.[136] Human life is a sharing in the divine life in and through Jesus Christ. After having seen that human life gets his meaning through Jesus Christ who is the truth, way, and life, he invites our attention to our actual condition of life. The meaning of our existence is totally in dependence on Christ. To arrive at a closer union with God one has to come with a closer union with Christ. It is through Christ that one reaches very close to God and becomes aware of himself.

---

132 Susan Muto, *John of the Cross for Today: The Dark Night*, p. 277.

133 Jordan Regis, "Jesus Christ in the Writings of John of the Cross", in *Carmelite Studies, John of the Cross: Conferences and Essays by Members of The Institute of Carmelite Studies and others*, p. 105.

134 John of the Cross, S .C. stz. 8:3 in Keiran Kavanaugh, Otilio Rodriguez, (tr.), *St. John of the Cross, Collected Works,* p. 441.

135 John of the Cross, S. C. stz. 12:8, in Keiran Kavanaugh, Otilio Rodriguez, (tr.), *St. John of the Cross, Collected Works,* p. 456.

136 Jordan Regis, "Jesus Christ in the Writings of John of the Cross", in *Carmelite Studies, John of the Cross: Conferences and Essays by Members of The Institute of Carmelite Studies and others*, p. 106.

Conclusion

In this chapter the logical and structural elements of our self, seen through the mind of John of the Cross is made evident. Five senses in the lower part of the soul are the gateways for going out and coming in. They gather information that are reflected in the interior faculties and later transformed into the principles that are food for the soul. In the higher part of the soul, mind or the interior faculties of intellect, memory and will takes the role of a bridle or hook in controlling and regulating the exterior senses for choosing the right and perfecting the soul where the soul can reach in setting its goal.

In the highest part or the centre of the soul, not many gateways are left for the entry within but only one which the Son of God enters. It is he who regulates the accesses of in and out and it is the sanctuary of our soul. Here the Spirit of God takes the control of our self and the devil cannot know how mysteriously God works in such souls who are submissive to God.

Art of learning this discernment right from the childhood would enable the persons to do the right and reject what is unfair. Often one works hard day and night, from the dawn of life as a child until the eve of the old age for the survival of one's own life and for the life of the beloveds. We fail even to think of the imperishable aspects within us and in our beloveds and cherish or sustain it. Right from the beginning of our childhood, we forget to see the needs of our mind or the mind of the other. We care normally only for the physical needs and our attention is often led only to satisfy the externalities alone. We forget and also fail to remind the other that we are creatures made with body, mind (intellect, memory, will) and Soul. Lives often ends and finishes with unexpected events, perishable gaining or momentary pleasures, failures or loses that are humanly impossible to set right, irretrievable or unattainable. Here neither children nor grownups are able to face the hazards of life, because from the early stages onwards we are not inculcated or attuned to get nourished from them with an outlook of a mystical dimension. It can be possible only with true knowledge that derives from devotion and faith. This happens with a realization that God sends each season to feed our physical, psychological and spiritual needs and that human impossibilities are God's possibilities. As we desire to protect our body from ill-health and weakness, it is necessary that we learn to protect our interior faculties as well. A chapter much focussed on these faculties are thus very apt here.

The analysis given at the end - Christ our way, truth and life in the light of John's spirituality will equip the traveller to a focussing point, journey with a guide, light, more relevance, meaning and a source of life. The narration of seven, eight, and ten steps given by John with the stages of mystical ladder, explanations on the winds, three theological virtues applied with each faculties, and the effects of Christ's love produced in the soul, and the effects of the Cross of Christ in restoring oneself, and the explanation on water sides and the features of river, etc., are real guidelines and support for anyone who stand perplexed by the strong winds and tempest in their life journey.

Word of God says that: "Do not give yourself over to sorrow, and do not distress yourself deliberately. A joyful heart is life itself, and rejoicing lengthens one's life span" (Sir 30:22), "Do not add to the troubles of the desperate, or delay giving to the needy" (Sir 4:3). This shows how we should be compassionate and gentle in dealing with our own mind when it is in anger or grief and the mind of others that are distressed by grief or anger. Just as we leave our bodies for healing with rest and medicine, we need to leave our minds too for its own healing and health by the time. Because, Christ the eternal One, the needle that regulate the time, can perfects everything with His own designs according to the season.

A plant produces good and healthy fruit, if it is properly brought up right from the beginning. Similar is the wisdom with which a human soul gets nurtured and matured. As in the case of child Jesus who grew and became strong, filled with wisdom; and with favour of God upon him (Lk. 2:40) we and our generation also should grow not only in physical power and strength but with divine wisdom in the interior faculties and God's favour at the centre of our soul.

We are eager to infill our children with all the knowledge that the world can provide, but often fail to feed them with the knowledge of their own self and how they are built or structured. We know that we are created and formed in the image and likeness of God. But, an effort to see the union and distinction of the Trinitarian God within us with the structural distinction and union of our faculties; that is how the body, mind and soul are distinct and at the same time one, may enable us to love ourselves with more perfection and wholeness.

By knowing our self through the spirituality of John, we are more closely entering into an integral awareness of our own self. Learning to live with Christ Jesus in communion with an ascetical way in overcoming these vices and affinitive way to grow in virtues which we have discussed in this chapter will be a form of digital means of self–integration and union with God by doing the will of God at every moment. Life in this world is a grace to experience and share the divine glory and holiness by a share in the power, wisdom and love of God. At the outset of our journey we may have only a taste of it, but possessing it is a gradual process of a spiritual growth through the ups and downs of our life ladder. One who begins this inward journey of self – integration should know the possibilities of threats within one's own self. We are aware of the enemies outside of us and inform everyone. But, often we are destroyed by the enemies within and stand helpless just because we become unable to calm our mind or make the intellect to understand the truth that is very tangible to all. Here is the relevance of beginning our departure by becoming aware of the obstacles and instilling oneself from the very beginning itself with the support of the protecting wall, the sheer divine grace.

For the one who has firm faith in God, everything in life; the minute thoughts or the great events, all in its totality carries with it a mystical dimension. In other words, for a believer who begins to learn from life, nothing becomes unwanted or meaningless and everything he makes use with the fire that profuse from Christ who purifies and inflames all. A soul that cultivates the art of attuning oneself with Christ and journeying with the Holy Trinity always possesses a presence and awareness of God being within and without him/her. This all-embracing presence of God teaches the soul the process of integration and transformation of oneself from natural to the supernatural. It is an art of learning to make the right discernment with a bridled will and heart in the presence of God, who is the sure observer of our mind.

Chapter 2

EZEKIEL'S VISION OF THE RENEWED TEMPLE A SPIRITUAL EXPLANATION

Introduction

God is the God of Power, Wisdom, and Love. We are all called to share this grace in His glory and holiness. Though these attributes are very distinct in their task, they are inseparable in essence. In the previous chapter, making use of the spiritual understanding of John of the Cross on the human person we started to know how human person is designed oneself in the lower, higher and highest levels. Here, in this second chapter we are interested in discussing how this structured man can live an organized life being aware of his full dignity. In order to enter into this organized or structured life, choice is for the one who is ready to stand at the gate of life with the measuring reed 'that is the nature or standard of Christ.'[137] This is a search that tries to re-discover this intrinsic strength, wisdom and love of God that is infused in its perfect manner into a soul where God dwells with His glory and holiness. God's Hand is the hand of power that liberates, His Mind is the mind of wisdom that redeems and His Heart is the heart of love that renews. For this understanding the main focus in

137 W.W. Battershall, "Ezekiel" in Joseph S. Exell, (ed.), *The Biblical Illustrator*, (Baker Book House, Grand Rapids, Michigan, 1977) pp. 504-506.

this chapter shall be on the vision of the renewed temple and its structure from the book of Prophet Ezekiel along with the writings of John of the Cross in special reference to this book. With a spiritual outlook on its spaces, steps, procedures in the temple, direction etc., we shall concentrate on the spiritual explanation in the light of the spirituality of John of the Cross.

2.1. The Vision of the Renewed Temple and its Background

Historically speaking, the book of Ezekiel is mainly concerned with the period of Israelites between the death of Josias in 609 and the destruction of Jerusalem in 587 B. C. Ezekiel was one of the deported along with king Joachin who surrendered to the Babylonians after three months of reign in 597 B. C.[138] Ezekiel's prophecies date after this event, probably from 593 B. C. The recipients of prophet's message were the split nations of Israel, (Israel and Judea) whose reunion happened in Babylon exile. Moreover, the prophet spent much of his time telling the exiles that Jerusalem would indeed fall (as it did happen later) and so they should not expect a quick return to their land. And instead of focusing their energy on the disastrous occurrences of exile, they should focus their energies on living in their new exilic context in obedience to the will of God. The theophany with the divine vision and vocation in the river bank of Chebar given at the beginning of the book reveals the role of the prophet Ezekiel. The vision of the new temple is derived with a message that Israel will be restored after she bears the judgment for her iniquity and rebellion, and where she will dwell securely with no one to cause her to tremble. Also, there will come a time when Israel will recognize Yahweh's sovereignty in her midst and Yahweh would pour out His Spirit upon Israel and never again will hide His face from her.[139] The New Temple vision explained in chapters 40-48 also reveals the accomplishment of a time where all covenants of Yahweh with Israel is fulfilled in the final restoration and Yahweh is returning to dwell in His sanctuary as their God for ever. This will be a testimony for all

138 E. Power, "Ezekiel" in *A Catholic Commentary on Holy Scripture*, (Thomas Nelson & Sons Ltd., London, 1955) pp. 601-602.

139 F. Edward Siegman, *The Book of Ezekiel*, (Paulist Press, New York, 1961) p. 68.

nations to recognize Yahweh's sovereignty as He sanctifies Israel by His presence for ever.[140]

2.1.1. The Immediate Context of Ezekiel's Temple Vision

According to the biblical studies the Vision of the restored temple occurred around 573 B. C.,[141] in the 25th year of exile, first of the year and the 10th day of the month (Ezek 40:1-4). In the light of the entire context of the book, the recipient of the vision is Ezekiel himself. He sensed the hand of Yahweh on him and in the vision, he was carried to a very high mountain in the land of Israel upon where he viewed the structure of a city on the south of the mountain. Ezekiel also observed a 'divine messenger', carrying a 'linen cord' and a 'measuring rod', who would be his guide and interpreter throughout the vision. Ezekiel was asked by this messenger to look closely, listen attentively and set his mind upon all that he is shown by him, for Ezekiel would be required to declare it to the house of Israel in the exile.[142] The architectural detail of the first section of the closing vision reaches its climax with the return of the glory to the new temple from the east gate. The renewed temple becomes the 'Throne' and the 'Footstool' of Yahweh and the 'law' of the temple is "holiness."[143]

2.2. Structure of the Renewed Temple

The Structure of the New Temple is made up of a triplet model that is 'Outer Court' (Ezek 40:17-31), 'Inner Court' (Ezek 40:32-47) and 'Temple Proper' (Ezek 40:48). Temple proper is again structured with 'Vestibule' (Ezek 40:48-49), 'Nave' (Ezek 41: 1-2), and 'Holy of Holies' (Ezek 41:3-4, 43:7-12).

---

140 Alexander Ralph, *Ezekiel*, (Moody Press, Chicago, 1978) p. 118.

141 Joseph Blenkinsopp, *Interpretation, A Bible Commentary for Teaching and Preaching* (John Knox Press, Louisville, 1990) pp. 4-5; J. Muilenburg, "Ezekiel", in *Peake's Commentary on the Bible*, (ed.) Mathew Black & H. H. Rowley, (Routledge, Taylor & Francis Group, London, 2001) p. 587.

142 Alexander Ralph, *Ezekiel*, pp. 136-137.

143 J. Muilenburg, "Ezekiel", in *Peake's Commentary on the Bible*, (Mathew Black & H. H. Rowley, (ed.), (Routledge, Taylor & Francis Group, London, 2001) p. 588.

i. Outer Court

Ezekiel is led into the outer court through the east gate. Outer court consists of its chambers and pavement all around the court. Then he examined the north gate, and south gate. And a flight of seven steps led to each gate situated to the north (Ezek 40:22), south (Ezek 40:24) and east (Ezek 40:26) sides of the outer court.

ii. Inner Court

Another flight of eight steps led to each of three gates similarly situated to the south (Ezek 40:31), east (Ezek 40:34), and north (Ezek 40:37) sides of the inner court. In the vestibule of this court took place the sacrifice of burnt offerings, sin offering, and guilt offering. Only Priests were admitted to this inner court. On the outside of the inner gateway of the inner court there were chambers for the singers. In the inner court, the highest level is the Temple Proper (Ezek 40:48–41:26).

iii. Temple Proper

The Temple Proper occupied a highest elevation. It comprised: Vestibule; Sanctuary and The Holy of Holies. Here the Prophet could find the High Mountain (Ezek. 43:7, 11-12).

a) The Vestibule/Ulam

There were the pilasters of the vestibule, 5 cubits on either side. The depth of the vestibule was 20 cubits and width 12 cubits. It raised ten steps above the inner court (40:48–49). The sacrifices of burnt offerings, sin offerings, and guilt offerings were taking place in this vestibule of the inner court.

b) Nave/Hekal

The nave had its pilasters, and the length of the nave was 40 cubits and its width 20 cubits (Ezek 41:1 – 2).

c) Sanctuary/The Holy of Holies

The inner room with its pilasters were of 2 cubits and the width 6 cubits. The depth of the room was 20 cubits and its width 20 cubits (41:3-4). And this is the inner room into which Ezekiel is lifted by the Spirit and was described to him as the place that is: 'Place of my Throne'(Ezek 43:7) and 'Top of the Mountain' (Ezek 43:12).

2.2.1. The Renewed Temple and its Representations

God's purpose of choosing Ezekiel as just and righteous in exercising His mission to the exiles, made himself not to rebel against God's message as would Israel, but accept and assimilate it without alteration before proclaiming it to the people of Yahweh. Being aware that he was called to be also a watchman for the house of Israel, he watched himself first being bound within his house (Ezek 4:4-15). The preparations for the divine vision in the beginning in the valley of Chebar amidst all afflictions must have been a lesson for him to fortify himself and to fix his wavering knee to the high mountain in order to concentrate intently, grasp, assimilate, give value and attention to all relevant or simple and even minute things which is visible to him. For the prophet it was not so easy to comprehend any of the visions which he had, such as the divine vision narrated in the beginning of his prophecy and later narrations of the temple visions in chs. 8-10, and chs. 40-48. The perplexities and complexities expressed during these experiences of the visions reveal how they influenced the life of the prophet himself. For him the first effect of the reception of the vision was a personalisation and integration of it in his own life. As he gave importance to the glory of Yahweh which was revealed to him in the divine vision, he was equally attentive in giving importance to the holiness of Yahweh. By getting a renewed temple for Israel being purified from all its filth, the prophet could dream to retain the Holy Name of Yahweh which was profaned among his people by their false witnessing (cf. Ezek 39:21-29). And the ascetic life of prophet himself is a witness how vigilant he was in preserving this glory and holiness of Yahweh in his life and how the vision of a renewed temple restored his life.

2.2.2. The Implications of the Renewed Temple in the Life of Israel

In the beginning the divine vision reveals the magnificent manifestation of the God of Israel who resided with His people in their temple from the very beginning.[144] But, without much delay the prophet could see the slaughtering in the city and the glory of the Lord leaving the threshold of the temple (cf. Ezek 9). The purpose of this revelation was for a renewed understanding of Yahweh. So, it was an appeal for renewal and renovation of their life in relationship with the commandment of Yahweh. First, God revealed Himself to a nation and people who didn't knew Him. To know Him as the 'only God' means to know Him through His power. Ezekiel was a prophet who recognized this power of God's Spirit Who raised him to stand on his feet and enabled him to hear the Word of Yahweh.[145] Throughout the Scripture God repeats that He is choosing, calling, specifying, empowering or arming and making Himself known to them though they do not know Him (cf. Is 45:4-6). Knowing God is to know His power, His attributes and strength. People of Israel believed that 'God's name as Power'- power to destroy the evil and to restore the good. They also had faith in 'God's name as Protection'- to protect the humble and to control the strong (Ps 44:5). Though God assured His almighty power to Israel and revealed Himself, they still strayed away and became feeble and helpless in knowing God (cf. Job 23:8-10).

In such a situation of dark den Prophet Ezekiel armed with faith, hope and love lead them to God. Prophet reminds them that the captivity and exile is the consequences of Israel's sin. The infidelity and disobedience to Yahweh's statutes and profanation of holy things, above all the temple and the Holy of Holies, where His glory dwelt were highlighted by the prophet. For him it is the profanation of Yahweh's holiness that which is the most heinous of all crime. The destruction of the temple and of Jerusalem obviously filled the minds of the exiles with great perplexity. But, the dominant theme of the final portion of the book of Ezekiel brings rays of hope, restoration and renewal of Israelites. Life germinated in the vision of the prophet that the nation is to rise from its death and destruction and the sons of Yahweh's servant David will be restored and the king will

---

144 Alexander Ralph, *Ezekiel*, (Moody Press, Chicago, 1978) pp. 134-35.

145 J. Muilenburg, "Ezekiel", in *Peake's Commentary on the Bible*, p. 570.

be Yahweh's prince for ever.[146] The temple vision of Ezekiel brings the joy of a people being purified. The promise of Yahweh in the wilderness that the people will be purified is being fulfilled here as the renewed temple of Ezekiel comes to its realization after the exile.

2.2.3. Vision of the Renewed Temple and the Inner Life of a Person

A close spiritual look into the vision of the structure of the temple can lead us to the following thoughts. Our life is structured like the temple in prophet's vision. The design of the structure is determined by the position of the stones.[147] As we are built upon the foundation of the apostles and prophets, with Christ Jesus himself as the cornerstone, we get the strategy as to the dignity that Christ imagined for us. In Jesus Christ the whole structure is joined together and grows into a holy temple in the Lord (cf. Eph. 2:20-21).

Holiness is always in touch with what is true and visible to our eyes, experienced with human senses. It is explicable and experiencing; and so is in relation with true emotions and feelings. Ezekiel's temple vision touched many people who were oppressed, deviated, alienated, and who were crushed. Though this vision never worked out as a blueprint for an actual temple[148] this vision could bring in them the strength, hope, love and zeal for their God Yahweh and keep themselves away from the alien gods and pagan cults. Having an open eye to see the mystical dimension of the vision of the new temple of Prophet Ezekiel with a very personal perspective can help many who are in the journey to holiness and take them

146 Ezek 37:24-26; J. Muilenburg, "Ezekiel", in *Peake's Commentary on the Bible*, p. 570.

147 W. W. Battershall "Ezekiel", in *The Biblical Illustrator* (ed.) Joseph Exell, pp. 504-506.

148 Lawrenec Boadt, "Ezekiel", in R. E. Brown, J. A Fitzmyer-R. E. Murphy, (ed.), *The New Jerome Biblical Commentary* (Bangalore: Theological Publications in India, 2004) p. 326.

to the high mountain "the holy of holies" with various degrees in holiness.[149]

Ezekiel chapters 3 and 4 are full of symbolic actions. Even the slightest actions in Ezekiel has a symbolic meaning (cf. Ezek 4:6). This symbolic aspects and mystical dimension of life has explored the future and restored temple with a new spring of spirituality. As such was the holy way the prophet continued in his life, the visions also followed him throughout the life. These visions lifted him from the valley (cf. Ezek 1:1; 3:22) to the high mountain (cf. Ezek 40:2) where God's hand rests (Is 25:10) and to the holy sanctuary where God resided. In all his visions he could feel the hand of God coming on him (cf. Ezek 1:3; 40:1) and when God's Hand rested in him, he was vested to work with God.

i. The Aspect of Mountain

In the book of Genesis, one sees the phrase "after the creation God rested" (cf. Gen 2:2-3). In the book of Isaiah, we read that God's hand rests in a Mountain (cf. Is 25:10). From these words it is evident that the people of that time thought that the resting place of God is up above in the mountain. At this point it is good to note that the divine vision of Prophet Ezekiel began from river bank of Chebar and ended it up with the temple vision in a high Mountain. Just like in the vision of Prophet Ezekiel starting from the valley and ending up on the high mountain, for John of the Cross the spiritual journey is like starting from the plane land and climbing through a ladder ascending to the Mountain for reaching Christ. John of the Cross in his book 'The Spiritual Canticle' tells that "The Son is the only delight of the Father, who rests nowhere else, nor is present in any other than in His Beloved Son. He rests wholly in His Son…."[150] Here Son becomes the Holy Mountain where God's hand rests and Son works. In the inner most being of our soul the Word, the Son of God, together with the Father and the Holy Spirit dwells hidden by

149 Joseph Blenkinsopp, *Interpretation, A Bible Commentary for Teaching and Preaching*, pp. 201-239.

150 John of the Cross, S. C. stz. 1:5, in Keiran Kavanaugh, Otilio Rodriguez, (tr.), *St. John of the Cross, Collected Works*, p. 417.

essence, grace and affection.[151] Our life journey is an inward journey towards this dwelling place. In this process, one need to preserve the soul in a state of tranquillity and equanimity by a withdrawal and detachment.[152] One could say that his life journey begins from a river bank that is the lower part of the soul. With mortifications, penances and spiritual exercises one practices in his sensual level and reaches a life to the high mountain where a virtuous life is lived controlled by the divine Spirit where, the rest of everything in the world was counted as unwanted and nothing.

ii. East Gate and Christ the Gate

Considering the future temple of Ezekiel, biblical exegetes bring out the mystical dimension of the shapes and measures, spaces, steps and measuring reed etc., of the temple. The new temple designs and forms are seen with a new meaning of holiness which can enrich anyone with more spiritual insights. In the Vision of the new temple of Ezekiel eastern gate becomes a gate to begin the journey and to progress (cf. Ezek 40:10) from the outer court to north and then to south in order to measure and inspect the northern and southern gates whether they are identical with the east gate in design and dimensions.[153] It is a gate where the glory of God stopped (cf. Ezek 10:19) and a gate through which prophet could see those who devise iniquity and who give wicked counsel (cf. Ezek 11:2) and also a gate for the Divine effulgence to re-enter into the temple (Ezek 43:4). It is also a closed gate because God our Lord has already entered through it. So "only the prince may sit in it to eat bread before the Lord; he shall enter by way of the vestibule of the gate", only for the prince to eat food before the Lord (cf. Ezek 44:3). It is a gate to be closed for six days of the week, to be opened for the Sabbath and the New Moon day (cf. Ezek 46:1), a gate for the prince to take his position by the doorposts of the gate as the priests offer his burnt offerings and his communion sacrifice (cf. Ezek 46:2).

---

151 John of the Cross, S. C. stz. 11:3, *Collected Works,* p. 449.

152 Peter Chakiath, *The Art of Unveiling the Spirit,* (Carmel International Publishing House, Trivandrum, 2015) p. 292.

153 Joseph Blenkinsopp, *Interpretation, A Bible Commentary for Teaching and Preaching,* pp. 201-239.

In the temple vision of Ezekiel only the prince enters through the eastern gate and he is siting to dine at table. According to John of the Cross, the only gate to enter into the fullness of God and to the riches of Him is the Cross of Christ.[154] This represents the gate that Jesus stood and suffered in order to sanctify the people by his own blood (cf. Heb 13:12; Jn 19:13). Christ is the prince and he alone is the gate way through which we can enter into this divine presence and sanctifying grace. As we grow in hope through Christ, our hope is redemptive. It is only beneath the tree of his cross there is restoration and redemption. As worshippers enter from the east and face the divine presence[155] it is a unique grace to begin our journey in and through Christ – the Way, the Truth and the Life. As Jerusalem is searched with lighted candles[156] only from the holiness of Christ, who is the light of the world, we can recognize our impurity. Christ the crucified is the *Todo* or everything for John of the Cross[157] on the way to the mountain and Christ is the point on which he is to be attached as the rest of everything in the life is *Nada* for him.

The wall around the temple area emphasizes the need to safeguard the enclosed space.[158] This wall takes us also to the beginning of a spiritual journey with which the prophet himself began his prophetic call where God himself is assigning the prophet to do as follows: "and put siege works against it, and build a siege wall against it, and cast up a ramp against it; set camps also against it, and plant battering rams against it all around" (Ezek 4:2). Divine power that flows through prayer and life of holiness is the protecting wall that resists the entry of profane. The only height measurement given[159] here can stand for the heavenly protection the soul gains

---

154 John of the Cross, S .C. stz. 36:13, in Keiran Kavanaugh, Otilio Rodriguez, (tr.), *St. John of the Cross, Collected Works*, p. 549.

155 Cf. Ezek 46:3, Joseph Blenkinsopp, *Interpretation, A Bible Commentary for Teaching and Preaching*, pp. 201-239.

156 John of the Cross, S. C, stz. 1:1, *Collected Works*, p. 416.

157 Peter Chakiathe, *The Art of Unveiling the Spirit*, p. 69.

158 Brian Boyle, "Holiness has a Shape" in *Australian Biblical Review*, 2008-09, Vol. 57, pp. 4-7.

159 Cf. Ezek 42:20; Joseph Blenkinsopp, *Interpretation, A Bible Commentary for Teaching and Preaching*, pp. 201-239.

before the journey in its initial operations. If the boundaries are protected well with the divine guards, the safety of the temple is assured. In today's world there are steps found everywhere to honour, riches, and worldly glory etc. One has to look at the steps to the sanctuary in the temple vision with this background. The steps by which men go up to the temple sanctuary is opposed to those which men take to their lusts and empty glories.[160]

Regarding the prince or Nasi: Nasi is presented as a central figure in Ezekiel's plan or the restored sacral sphere, where he is to function as the primary lay worshiper and cult patron in the prophet's theocratic vision of society.[161] The reign of nasi represents no more violence, oppression, no enforce, but everything is according to just weights and measures, i.e., everything according to its proper manner.[162] Regarding the prince, it is also said that the line of Yahweh's servant David will be restored and the king will be Yahweh's prince for ever (cf. Ezek 37:24-26). Christ in the line of David is now reigns as the only king who is the king and prince of peace fulfilling all the prophecies in Him.[163]

While gateways and entrances provide access, they also serve as barriers, thus determining spheres of holiness and a gradual sense of protection with these spheres. The concern of space and shape is to define and protect the sphere of the holy from the contagion of the profane.[164] A life mortified in external senses will serve as an access or provider to the holiness as well as a barrier to the profane.

Regarding the offerings: particular terminology used in the text with regard to the ritual of purification of the altar apart from

---

160 John Bunyan "Ez 40:49: And he brought me by the steps, whereby they went up to it", in Joseph Exell S, (ed.), *Ezekiel, The Biblical Illustrator*, (Baker Book House, Grand Rapids, Michigan, 1977) p. 508.

161 Brian Boyle, "Holiness has a Shape": The place of the Altar in Ezekiel's visionary plan of Sacral Space (Ez 43:1-12, 13-17, 18-27) in *Australian Biblical Review*, 2008-09, Vol. 57, p -21.

162 Joseph Blenkinsopp, *Interpretation, A Bible Commentary for Teaching and Preaching*, p. 201.

163 J. Muilenburg, "Ezekiel", in *Peake's Commentary on the Bible*, p. 570.

164 Brian Boyle, "Holiness has a Shape": in *Australian Biblical Review*, 2008-09, Vol. 57, p. 6.

'to purify' and 'purification offering' emphasises the 'offering of purification' rather than 'sin offering' or expiation of sin.[165] A life lived in three theological virtues and life of mortifications and penances will free us from the imperfections of life as God is the sure observer of our mind and a true penitent receives grace from the mercy of God. The life in these virtues will also enable our whole self to offer as a living sacrifice in Christ to God the Father.

Regarding the measuring reed (Ezek 40:3) there are certain things which, fall entirely within our choice, which have such power and influence in the shaping of our character that they become the measuring reeds of life. They are man's estimate of himself, philosophy of life and the theory of life.[166] For John of the Cross in the ascend to the mountain of inner self, there was only one single light that enlightened the whole self, that is Christ and his life principles. The attitude of Christ on every little and great facts of life is the only perfect standard or theory that we can imitate in life. The length and heights of our life structure is the immeasurable length and the height of Christ whose measure is eternal and stable in goodness. It is His Beloved Son who will be the measuring reed with whose life Father can measure and identify his flocks and make His dwelling in them.

Prophet Ezekiel in his temple vision explains the purpose of describing the temple at first as to make the Israelites ashamed of their iniquities (cf. Ezek 43:10). Never a description of the material temple can bring shame to a person. It is the mighty divine influence that entirely changes the soul with a disposition of shame[167] and in the shadow of divine light the true penitent sees his ugly image with a clear vision.

---

165 Brian Boyle, "Holiness has a Shape": *in Australian Biblical Review*, 2008-09, Vol. 57, pp. 13-14.

166 W.W. Battershall, "Ezekiel", in *The Biblical Illustrator* (ed.), Joseph Exell S, (Baker Book House, Grand Rapids, Michigan, 1977) pp. 504-506.

167 John Love, "If they be ashamed of all that they have done", in Joseph Exell S, (ed.), *Ezekiel, The Biblical Illustrator*, (Baker Book House, Grand Rapids, Michigan, 1977) pp. 504-506.

2.3. Life Structure and Living Temple in the Light of John's Spirituality

God who is Holy fashioned us in His own image and we are ought to be the dwelling place of God structured with respective properties for proposed functions. Each portion bears their own dignity and duty, yet they are asked to be controlled and formed to obey the command of God in love. The Following part of the spiritual explanation on the renewed temple structure will be an analysis on human life structure in the light of the spirituality of John of the Cross.

2.3.1. Outer Court (Ezek 40:19-31) at Lowest Level

It was through the east gate that the prophet entered into the outer court. Outer court consists of its chambers and pavement all around the court. Then he inspected the north gate, and the south gate. And a flight of seven steps led to each gates situated to the north (Ezek 40:22), south (Ezek 40:24) and east (Ezek 40:26) sides of the outer court. For John of the Cross, lower part of the soul is our external senses and they are the gateways to pass information from outer self to the inner as well as from inner self to the outer just as the east, north and south gateways work in the temple structure of Ezekiel. Though there is the divine providence and protection for the chosen race, yet there can be unmeasured sufferings a purifying soul has to face on its way to the transformation in the realm of senses which are always in touch with the open world. The sound in the ear and the knowledge in the spirit is an effect of the material voice.[168] Similarly, the role of the outer court of senses in gathering food for the soul is very important in the adventure of inner journey. How hard they work for the food in this outer court with the support of senses depends upon the intensity of holiness that each soul need to progress. The following part will analyse the stages and effect of this elevation to holiness with the support of the steps mentioned in the journey to the sanctuary.

---

168 John of the Cross, S. C. stz. 14, 15:10, in Keiran Kavanaugh, Otilio Rodriguez, (tr.), *St. John of the Cross, Collected Works,* p. 466.

i. The Steps from the Outer Court

The temple vision of Ezekiel points out several steps from outer court to enter into the temple proper. The increasing elevation brought the person nearer to the holy and transcendent God who is in the inner most centre. Through this concept Ezekiel reveals that it is not enough only to be separated from the profane but need to climb the degrees of perfection. The steps or the degrees on the way are: From inner front of the lower gate to the outer front of the inner court a flight of several steps led to each gate situated to the east (Ezek 40:6). Then he went into the gateway facing east, going up its steps, and measured the threshold of the gate, one reed deep. Here the striking point is that the east way does not mention how many steps are there exactly to climb. Just as the east side of the outer court does not mention exact number of the steps to be climbed; John of the Cross narrates that in the beginning, in order to lift the soul from the extreme of its low state to the other extreme of the high state of divine union, do so with order, gently and according to the mode of the soul. An exact or compulsory method or manner in spiritual growth is not instructed here. Naturally or Supernaturally, God brings a person to the supreme Spirit of God in faith by any experiences of his gentle touch of healing, or any other experiences through various means according to the individual's own manner of acquiring knowledge.[169]

ii. Seven Steps (Ezek 40:20-26) at North and South

Standing at the outer court itself, one needs to cleanse the base level of one's knowledge the intellect. As the porch of the outer court is at the inner end (cf. Ezek. 40:20-22), one's sensuality works according to one's basic understanding that the intellect holds. In an inordinate soul there is a deposit of intense filth and degradation as the variety of its appetites for creatures.[170] It is good to remember here the narration of the prophet that he saw all kinds of crawling reptiles and all the abomination of unclean animals painted on the interior walls

169 John of the Cross, A. II. Ch. 17:3-4, in Keiran Kavanaugh, Otilio Rodriguez, (tr.), *St. John of the Cross, Collected Works* , p. 156.

170 John of the Cross, A. I. Ch. 9, *Collected Works,* p. 91.

of the temple (cf. Ezek. 8:10-16). This interior wall of the temple could be seen as a representation of the human faculties.

The intellect is the first chamber characterizing intellectual thoughts of abject earthly things and of all creatures. This can be the evil that happens in our rational faculties or in intellect. The evil influences have to be renounced. This is represented as the North wind and evils of this north wind is deadening for the soul because it extinguishes the satisfaction, delight and fragrance of the virtues the soul enjoys. Habitual denial and repentance of these appetites has to be practiced with faith by dark night of senses, purifying oneself of their residue.[171] The means to purify this is faith, and for the intellect faith is dark night.[172]

The reptiles in the outer court of the castle are human animalistic nature and instincts. If they are unchecked, they entangle and we become cruel, jealous, greedy, violent, worldly, absorb in worldly affairs, honours, ambitions and indulge in false values etc. We are to withdraw from such vanities and can never love until we control our passions.[173]

This is a ladder and by stepping upwards one learns to get deprived of the pleasure from all temporal benefits and gaining. The main advantage of this stepping is the self-purification. At the starting point, the soul is more concentrated on one's own satisfaction and self-centeredness. Hence, the growth in this stage of self-denial effects to the perfection of one's own soul and the acts of renunciation is also motivated towards the growth of self. The soul here advances in the virtue of faith, hope and love yet this love does not shine in the extreme of suffering for the other as it suffers for the salvation of oneself (cf. Ezek 14:13-14).

This is a stage where a deprivation, desolation and spiritual aridity is experienced (cf. Ezek 5:12). Such people becomes very slack in charity toward God and neighbour, as the self-love contained in their works makes them grow cold in charity. According to John of

171 John of the Cross, A. I. Ch. 5:7, in Keiran Kavanaugh, Otilio Rodriguez, (tr.), *St. John of the Cross, Collected Works,* p. 83.

172 John of the Cross, A. I. Ch. 2:1, *Collected Works*, p. 74.

173 Teresa of Avila, *Interior Castle*, E. Allison Peers, (tr. & ed.), (Image Books, New York, 1972) p. 31.

the Cross this is the stage where one needs to overcome seven steps of self–abnegation in order to grow in charity.[174] The seven steps proposed by John of the Cross are the following:

a) One need to avoid vanity, pride, vainglory and presumption.
b) Self-esteem which follows with a contempt for others and getting envious when noticing the praise others receive.
c) Performing the task with the expectation of gratification or praise.
d) Seeking joy, comfort, honour or similar things in this life itself.
e) The attachment in seeking satisfaction and consolation in the works that discourages to persevere the way of perfection.
f) The evil of self-seeking and consolations in the works.
g) Need of overcoming the inhibition in taking counsels and receiving reasonable instructions.

For a leap from this world of sense to the more interior castle of God, one needs to eradicate these creatures of self–love while climbing from the outer court itself.

2.3.2. Inner Court (Ezek. 40:32-47) at Higher Level

This is the court which is occupied with outstanding events of a temple: such as the sacrifices and offerings, singing-an important form of worship etc. In the vestibule of this court took place the sacrifices of guilt offering, sin offering and grain offering. Only Priests were admitted to this inner court. On the outside of the inner gateway there were chambers for the singers in the inner court. There are three gates similarly situated heading towards the south, east, and north sides of the inner court and there are eight steps leading to each of these gates. On its journey from inner front of the inner court to outer front of the Temple proper there are eight

174 John of the Cross, A. III. Ch. 28, in Keiran Kavanaugh, Otilio Rodriguez, (tr.), *St. John of the Cross, Collected Works* (Carmel International Publishing House, Trivandrum, Kerala, 2006) p. 262.

steps to climb from each gate. In the inner court, the highest level is the Temple proper (cf. Ezek 40:48 – 41:26). The Temple proper occupies a higher elevation. It comprises Vestibule; The sanctuary; The Holy of Holies.

2.3.3. Elevation of 8 Steps: An In-depth Journey to Holiness

On its Journey from inner front of the inner court to outer front of the Temple proper there are eight steps to climb from each gates. Inner court by the south gate – stairway 8 steps: (cf. Ezek. 40:28-31); Inner court by the east side-stairway 8 steps: (cf. Ezek. 40:32-34); Inner court by the north gate–stairway 8 steps (cf. Ezek. 40:35-37). When one goes through the above said passages can observe the narration of many elevations and steps found to the sanctuary of the Lord in the temple seen by Ezekiel. As the sanctuary was found at the top of the mountain, the steps are ascending steps. This shows that in the process of ascending there will be something to leave behind as the traveller passes every step to possess the great. When one enters from the outer court to inner, though there are much to renounce, actually these renouncement's motivations are the possession of the greater. These steps are means of growth in holiness through faith, hope and charity.

John of the Cross refers that in an inordinate soul according to the variety of its appetites for creatures there is degradation and a deposit of intense filth. For the John of the Cross, the intellect[175] is the first chamber representing intellectual thoughts of abject earthly things and of all creatures.[176] He quotes here an excellent figure of these varied appetites from Ezekiel (cf. Ezek. 8:10-16). God showed the prophet all kinds of crawling reptiles and all the abomination of unclean animals painted on the interior walls of the temple.

'Warm winds blows from the South':[177] These words represent the stage of purification for the salvation of one's own soul. Here all the sufferings, desolation and purgation the soul undergoes will

175 John of the Cross, A. II. Chs. 2-151, pp. 109-149.

176 John of the Cross, A. I. ch. 9, p. 91.

177 Smith J., Acworth A., Hemer C. J, "Wind", *The Illustrated Bible Dictionary*, Part 3, (ed.) Parable-Zuzim, Mary Gladstone (et. al), (Tyndale House Publishers, UK, 1980) p. 1647.

be sufficient only to save enough one's own self (cf. Ezek. 14:15-16). First and the chief benefit of this dry and dark stage is the knowledge and recognition of the truth about its misery, of which it was formerly ignorant. Just as the south wind warms up everything, the intellect here receives the warmth of every new understanding. The following are the benefit of this stage: First, the soul learns to communes with God more respectfully and courteously.[178] As the self-knowledge flows from this dry night, there proceeds the other knowledge of God. Looking at Christ, the soul learns to love God with a pure love in the following manner:

a) A selfless God in Christ giving Himself as the best (cf. Jn 10:11).
b) God as a guard in Christ not to observe sins but to save and protect (cf. Mt 9:13).
c) God as a saving lion in Christ to save souls from the mouth of evil (cf. Jn 16:33).
d) God who renews our strength in Christ and will sprout wings like eagles (cf. Is 40:31; Jn 14:12).
e) God who works with him in Christ not leaving him alone to work like an ox (cf. Jn 14:13-14, 18).

In this stage a person also procures spiritual humility by overcoming the pride. The thought of being more advanced than others does not even occur in its first movements, as it did before; on the contrary, the soul realizes that others are better.[179] Even in this stage the soul is in the process of reaching to the mountain top, i.e., it is still in the progression towards the perfection of grace and charity. The person here also becomes submissive and obedient in the spiritual journey. The wretchedness of self makes the person to listen to the teachings of others and even desire to be directed by anyone.

i. The East Side

Considering the climatic conditions, the East winds earlier in the year often work great destruction on vegetation (cf. Ezek. 17:10).

178 John of the Cross, D N. I. ch. 12: 3, p. 322.

179 John of the Cross, D N. I. ch.12: 5-7, p. 323.

Under their influence strong plants droop, and flowers quickly wither (cf. Ps 103:16). The Prophet says that when he obeyed the command of God to enter further, he saw women siting and weeping for Adonis, the god of love, and behold greater abominations. Here the reflections of John of the Cross found in the *Ascend of the Mount Carmel* on the second chamber the will[180] is important.There are some appetites that come very gently but returns after great destruction on our life when left un-mortified.[181] These appetites weep as it were by coveting what the will is attached to, that is, they covet the reptiles painted in the intellect. This is a stage where God curbs concupiscence and bridles the appetites that the soul cannot feast any sensory delight from earthly or heavenly things (cf. Ezek. 14:17-18).

After this kind of purgation, the passions lose their strength and become sterile from not receiving any satisfaction. As the appetites and concupiscence are quenched the following effects derives: The soul lives in spiritual peace, tranquillity and consolation; the soul bears a habitual remembrance of God, accompanied by a fear and dread of turning back on the spiritual road; the soul in these steps of arid night exercises all the virtues together and persevere spiritual exercises without consolation or satisfaction in its work, but only by God. The soul here practices corporally and spiritually all the theological as well as cardinal and moral virtues. Still there are steps to be climbed in order to reach the mountain top in its perfection of grace and charity.

ii. The North Side

Just as the north wind turns up everything, the memory takes us away from the present and makes everything of the present to be still and allows the person to look back or to live in the past instead of travelling to the right reason, God Himself (cf. Ezek 8:16). For John, these men in the third room represents the images of creatures we preserves in the memory and reflects upon. With a wounded memory and negative mind, no one can have a right understanding of God or man. God generally sends storms and trials (cf. Ezek 1:4; 14:19-20)

180 John of the Cross, A. I. ch. 9, p. 93,

181 John of the Cross, A. I. ch, 8:6-7, p. 91.

in this sensory night and purgation, thus chastised and buffeted; the senses and faculties may be gradually exercised, prepared and inured for the union with wisdom which will be granted there. For if a soul is not tempted, tried and proved through temptations and trials, its senses will not be strengthened in preparation for wisdom. Here the soul undergoes the kind of purgation according to God's will and the greater or lesser amount of imperfection that must be purged from each one. In the measure of the degree of love to which God wishes to raise a soul, He humbles it with greater or less intensity, or for a longer or shorter period of time.[182]

Through baptism we are raised to a supernatural order where we are able to live a life of union with God. And if we do not advance in this realm of grace without negation of everything that prevents us from being God-like[183] we remain static in our intention to be perfect as Heavenly Father is perfect. The above-mentioned stages are really an entry to a life of royal priesthood which need courage. Only the souls who are courageous enough to pass beyond the interior and exterior limits of his nature are called to enter within these supernatural bounds of the royal priesthood where much more offerings and sacrifices are done again (1Pet 2:9).

2.4. Temple Proper: at the Highest Level (Ezek. 40:48)

Temple proper occupied a three-spaced elevation. It comprised of vestibule, nave and holy of holies or the sanctuary. The measurement of the room exposes a proportioned balance or equilibrium (Ezek. 41:3-4). This is the inner room into which Ezekiel is lifted by the Spirit and described to him as the place that is: 'Place of my Throne' (cf. Ezek. 43:7) 'Top of the Mountain' (cf. Ezek. 43:12).

Though not as a comparison, John of the Cross explains the measure and intensity of the further stage of the Holy of Holies or the centre of the soul in its degree of love by referring to the river vision.[184] It is sufficient for the soul to possess one degree of love,

---

182 John of the Cross, D N. I 14:4, p. 328.

183 Peter Bourne, *St. John of the Cross and the Dark Night*, (Wenzel Press, CA, 1993), p. 41.

184 "And further, deep into the thicket", (Cf. John of the Cross, S C, 36:10).

for by one-degree alone ankle deep (cf. Ezek. 47:3) it is united with Him through grace. Should it have two degrees, knee deep (cf. Ezek. 47:4) it will have become united and concentrated in God in another deeper centre. Should it reach three, up to the waist (cf. Ezek. 47:4) it will have centred itself in a third. But, once it has attained the final degree, God's love will have arrived at wounding the soul in its ultimate and deepest centre, which is to transform and clarify it in its whole being, power and strength, and according to its capacity, until it appears to be God.[185]

2.4.1. Increasing Demand of Holiness: Elevation through 10 Steps

Despite Israel's past and present, Yahweh would bring Israel once more into the wilderness and purge the rebels from out of its midst. This is a departure of the intellect for a change from human and natural to the divine. And it is a departure of the will from its lowly manner and natural strength to the strength and purity of the Holy Spirit. It also is a change of memory into the presentiments of eternal glory.

These steps are more oppressive night of the spirit in order to reach the divine union of love, because not everyone but only a few usually reach this union as this night is ordinarily accompanied by burdensome trials and sensory temptations which last for a long time (cf. Ezek 14:21-23). This is a purgation effected from an inflow of God's love into the soul, which purges it of its habitual ignorance and imperfections which are natural and spiritual. This divine light is a dark night because of the height of the divine wisdom which exceeds the capacity of the soul. Another aspect is that the soul's baseness and impurity make it feel painful and afflictive as the hand of God touches it to grant favours, not to chastise it.[186]

The soul feels here that God has rejected it in the shadow of death, abandoned by all creatures and friends, and also feels its own intimate poverty and misery. Since these imperfections are deeply

185 John of the Cross, L F, 1:9-17, pp. 582-586.

186 John of the Cross, D N. II Ch 5, p. 335.

rooted in the substance of the soul, it also suffers an oppressive undoing and an inner torment (cf. Ezek. 24:10-11).[187]

Besides all these intense burning, the fire of love always rises only upwards as though longing to be engulfed in its centre. While annihilating all imperfections and filth this living flame of love elevates the soul to its deepest centre of love.[188] This love will enable the soul to accommodate everyone along with her in this journey to the Sanctuary of the Lord. Charity blooms here and the soul will be saved with escorts of her beloveds (cf. Ezek 14:22).

2.4.2. The Theological Virtues as Garments to Sustain the Holiness[189]

The priest uses a type of garments when he is in the sanctuary. Here, in the vision describes on the importance of putting on other garments when the priest goes to the outer court. It is to protect them from communicating the holiness to people and being exhausted of grace due to the contact with the outer world. John of the Cross uses the term 'disguised' and describes with a relevant meaning by attributing the colours for this garment the soul wears in this night.[190] According to him a person disguises himself by fortifying against its three enemies, the world, flesh and the devil. He then chooses the garments and livery which most represent and signify his heart's affections and with which he can better dissemble himself from his enemies. Touched with love for Christ, it's Spouse, and aspiring to win His favour and friendship, the soul departs in the disguise that more vividly represents the affections of its spirit. Its advance in this disguise makes it more secure against its adversaries; the world, the flesh, and the devil. John of the Cross identifies the dress it wears with three principal colours: White, Green, and Red. These three colours stand for the three theological virtues: Faith, Hope, and Charity.

187 John of the Cross, D N. II Ch 6:5, p.339.

188 John of the Cross, D N. II. Ch. 20:6, pp. 377-8.

189 Ezek 44:19.

190 John of the Cross, D N. II. Ch. 21, p. 378.

i. Faith (White)

Faith is an inner tunic of such pure whiteness that it blinds the sight of every intellect. When the soul is clothed in faith, the devil is ignorant of how to hinder it, neither is he successful in his efforts. To obtain the favour of the Beloved and union with Him, the soul can have no better inner tunic than this white garments or virtues. Without faith it is impossible to please God (cf. Heb. 11:6) The soul wore this white tunic of faith when it departed on this dark night and walked in the midst of interior darkness and straits, without the comfort of any intellectual illumination neither from above, because heaven seemed closed and God hidden and nor from below.

ii. Hope (Green)

The soul over this white tunic of faith puts on a second colour garment, a green coat. Green signifies the virtue of hope, by which one in the first place is defended and freed, as before from the second enemy, the world. Soul will be elevated to the things of eternal life and in comparison with this heavenly hope all earthly things seem dry, withered, dead, and worthless. He lives clothed only in the hope of eternal life. Hope covers all the senses so that they do not become absorbed in any worldly thing, nor is there any way in which some arrows from the world might wound them. Hope allows the soul only a visor that it may look toward heavenly things and no more. Without this green livery of hop in God alone, he would obtain nothingin this journey towards the goal of love, since what moves and conquers is unrelenting hope. The soul advances through this dark and secret night in the disguise of the green livery of hope, since it walks along so empty of all possession and support that neither its eyes nor its care are taken up with anything but God.

iii. Charity (Red)

Over the white and green, as the finishing touch and perfection of this disguise, the soul puts on a third colour which is a precious red toga. This colour denotes charity, the third virtue, which not only adds elegance to the other two colours but so elevates the soul as to place it near God. Charity makes it so beautiful and pleasing to

God. With this livery of charity, a livery of love, which increases love for the Beloved, the soul receives protection and concealment from the flesh, its third enemy. For where there is true love of God, love of self and of one's own things finds no entry. Not only does charity protect it, but it even makes the other virtues genuine, strengthens and invigorates them in order to fortify the soul, and bestows on them loveliness and charm so as to please the Beloved thereby. For without charity no virtue is pleasing to God. The soul is clothed in this red livery when it departs in the dark night from itself and from all creatures, fired with love's urgent longings, and advances by the secret ladder of contemplation to perfect union with God who is its beloved salvation. These colours are a most suitable preparation for union of the three faculties, intellect, memory and will with God.

2.4.3. Dining with Christ the Prince in Solitude and Peace

"The Lord said to me: This gate shall remain shut; it shall not be opened, and no one shall enter by it; for the Lord, the God of Israel, has entered by it; therefore, it shall remain shut. Only the prince, because he is a prince, may sit in it to eat food before the Lord; he shall enter by way of the vestibule of the gate, and shall go out by the same way" (Ezek 44:2-3). In the above-mentioned passage, the prince of whom Ezekiel speaks is the prince of peace. When the people of the land come before the Lord, he comes in with them and when they go out, he goes out with them. In his temple vision the prince does not take any of the inheritance of the people. He gives his sons their inheritance out of his own holdings. Thus no one is dispossessed of their holding. The holy portion with the Sanctuary of the temple in the middle of it and the property of the Levites and the city, is in the middle of that which belongs to the prince. The prince in Ezekiel is firmly hemmed in by limitations. The prince is no longer the cornerstone of Israelite society; he is subject to the Law. It is true that the promised prince of the future temple is found as the heir of David the promised Messiah (Ezek 46:10, 18; 48:21–22). It is apt to find the prince who is firmly hemmed in by limitations of human nature under the law through the words of St. Paul's in his letter to the Galatians, "But when the fullness of time had come, God sent his Son, born of a woman, born under the law" (Gal 4:4).

Throughout the writings of John of the Cross only one single ray brightening the whole atmosphere is Christ the Crucified. Just as only the prince is allowed to enter and dine in the temple through the closed gate in Ezekiel's new temple, John of the Cross affirms that Christ is the only light to enter into the soul in its dark night.[191]

In order to enter into the dark night and ascent to the mountain, the soul needs to shut the door towards everything except Christ the Crucified. He alone is allowed to enter into the innermost room of the soul. The soul must burn only for the Beloved, in an unknown way along the road of solitude. He says that when everything regarding the earthly and heavenly things are put to sleep and in silence, the Divine Wisdom unites Himself with the soul in a new bond of the possession of Love. Thus, Christ has all the dazzling nature of the promised prince who alone sit and eat with the hungry soul in its dense dark night. And he himself is the Wisdom of God who found his dwelling place, the future temple, the hearts of human beings. Here the words of John of the Cross from the Spiritual Canticle is worth noticing:

"*Beneath the apple tree:*
There I took you for My own,
There I offered you My hand,
And restored you,
Where your mother was corrupted."[192]

The fruit bearing apple tree mentioned in the above said verses is the Cross of Christ, beneath which the corrupted nature of human person gets redeemed and restored. The gradual growth and perfection of the soul after the espousal in baptism is symbolically expressed by the saint with the support of the verses from the book of Ezekiel where the stages of a soul from birth up to growth are symbolically expressed.[193] In short, a life in grace with Christ, cherished by the fruit of his life-giving tree of the Cross is a source of the living water.

191 "With no other light or guide Than the one that burned in my heart", (Cf. John of the Cross, *Dark Night*, II. Ch. 25) p. 388.

192 John of the Cross, S. C. stz. 23, p. 499.

193 John of the Cross, S. C. stz. 23: 6, p. 500.

Conclusion

Mystical theology affirms that not all souls travel by the same route, but essentially it is the same journey that everyone is called to make. The journey along with John of the Cross to the renewed temple of Prophet Ezekiel reveals that the steps in the temple and the invitation of the guide from outer court to the inner sanctuary, is an indication that we all are invited (every human being, Israelites, the chosen people through baptism) to make an inner journey. It includes a life of purification of exterior and interior senses, illumination of interior faculties with the divine wisdom and union of our will with the divine will through the practice of theological virtues by which a soul is getting matured to reach God in the summit of self. This chapter unveiled the features of this journey a bit more visible and concrete to us. After understanding the nature and structure of man (the inner person) in the first chapter we were analysing the structure of the temple and its functional aspects as envisioned by Ezekiel the prophet. Since it is a vision one can naturally make out that it speaks symbolically something other than what it is described. Seen from the history and life of Israelites one can naturally deduce that its implications are connected with the inward journey of a community and of course of a person who is aspiring for a God oriented life.

The background of the vision of the renewed temple takes us to where we get the picture of Israelites who were in an exilic hope for their return to the homeland. This background history reveals that, though in an exile land, how Israel could recover her lost structure as a nation from the split form through her exilic background and how Israel was formed through prophet for the acceptance of divine will even in the context of deportation. It also reveals how Israel was formed by the prophet to bear judgments for their own iniquities and rebellion after which Israel will dwell securely with no one to cause her to tremble. Also, it invokes a time when Yahweh would pour out His Spirit upon her and never again would hide His face from her. It affirms that the new temple vision is recognition of Yahweh's sovereignty as He sanctifies and restores Israel by His presence for ever. This restoring picture of Israel through her exilic experience is very apt for getting a similar outlook in spiritual journey where soul who is a captive to the body may get a restoration and renewal when it recognizes sufferings as salvific.

The context of Ezekiel's temple vision given in this chapter takes us to the relevance of the prophetic mission given to Ezekiel and the impact of a guide or divine messenger who carried the linen cord and a measuring rod with which the entire vision is interpreted. And it also reveals the qualities a prophet should have such as by looking closely, listening attentively, and setting mind upon all that is shown. This part is concluded with the point where the glory of God is returned to the renewed temple from the east gate along with a notification of the renewed temple as the 'throne' and 'footstool of Yahweh' and the 'law' of the temple as 'holiness.' This context also foretells how a prophetic mind in our journey can enable us to look closely, listen attentively, and set mind upon all that is seen and experienced in life as a prophetic message; if we have Christ with us as our divine messenger along with his own life as linen cord and a measuring rod.

This temple structure along with many features of the temple and the ritual functions etc., provides more information for a life traveller to live an organized life that set one for a well-equipped sojourn. John of the Cross in his spiritual analysis of the structure of man and the temple structure found that there are striking similarities between both of them. Both could be understood as an inward journey or a spiritual journey of man. A clear example is the reflections of John of the Cross given on the vision on abominations done in the temple with the comparison of filth that gets rooted in the interior faculties of intellect, memory and will along with the comparisons of winds and its transformed forms as the person approaches to the mount so on, as they are very revealing for a soul that prepares for a task of spiritual expedition.

The steps with its elevation in degrees of holiness which are very identical and supportive in our inward journey of purification, illumination and union of will with the divine will by attaching ourselves to the light of Christ and His wisdom along with the steps and ladder explained by John of the Cross are very relevant for anyone who wish to progress in the spiritual life.

All are called to travel towards the truth, but truth is found not by doing an outward journey in spiritual aspects, rather entering into the fullness of one-self by finding God Who dwells within. In order to reach this peak point of grace, all are obliged to pass beyond the steps of all the natural theories, philosophies and understandings by surrendering one's intellect, memory and will to the perfect knowledge and wisdom that comes from Christ the crucified. The guiding light in this journey is Christ and the footstep that helps us to pass over our journey is the theory or the philosophy that we get while attuning our life with the mind and the attitude of Christ our guide.

The centrality of Christ in the renewal of our life is revealed by the analysis done on the 'east gate' and the cross of Christ. Often Christ is set aside by the title of religion and neglects the universal aspect as a guard and protector of human soul by the shedding of His blood once for all which is the only manner and ransom in saving the souls from the bondage of evil. The theory that John of the Cross followed while climbing the mount was of '*Neti*' or 'nothing'. He might have taken this aspect from his master Christ himself because Christ in conquering the head of Satan and ascending to heaven assumed the manner of self – emptying. The mention of sacrifices of various kinds (sin offerings, guilt offerings and grain offerings) by Prophet Ezekiel in entering into the sanctuary of the temple of God also a prefiguration of the self-emptying preferred for the one who wish to lead an inner life in God. Thus, all these aspects lead us to a similar conclusion that is - a path of renunciation is necessary in gaining oneself. Here gaining means gaining our souls from the clutches of evil inclinations that follow us always. The power of a perfect soul is the power of heaven and attaining this stage of perfection was the demand Jesus kept before us through the words "Be perfect, therefore, as your heavenly Father is perfect" (Mt 5:48).

For the Prophet Ezekiel finding God in life's journey and having a divine vision was not a desert experience or an island life. He found the powerful hand and presence of God while being with the people of Yahweh in their exile in Chebar valley and at the sanctuary of their dream temple. His God came to him after an experience like that of a deadening north wind that he experienced while being with them. Though he was isolating himself from the human desires of his self-satisfactions by an ascetic way of life, he was realistic and was not away from the sufferings of his people, the exiled ones. It was the same thing that Christ lived by being with the chosen ones; he attuned his will to the will of the Father through a self-renunciation. It means finding an island within oneself with a God who comes to us in a unique way; keeping our soul away from all the natural tendencies and sinfulness; accepting the other as they are; which are the ways to reach the glorious and holy mountain proposed by John of the Cross.

The explanation by the prophet regarding 'putting on other garments while going out from the sanctuary to the people' and the explanation given by John of the Cross on the three colours of disguised forms by separating them with three theological virtues germinates in us the confidence of perfecting our mentality with faith, hope and love. It is a process of getting confidence in a God who show concern towards us very personally and shaping our life with a secret love and growing in a unique outlook in divine providence. Though it is a journey to the Holy Sanctuary, arriving through the structured and disciplined entries, there is also a process of coming back to the same gates after having a vision of glorious and holy God. But, further journey will be a different and unique one because here while looking back, the soul will not be like the twenty-five old men whose backs were turned on the temple, but they will have a temple to look back and see from where a stream flowed eastwards from under the temple threshold, for the temple faced east, where the real prince took the possession of his place within the soul. At this stage the soul will be able to evaluate his/her life with a right discernment, and the principles formed from this right discernment will lead to a right decision, and the outcome of it is the outflow of this life-giving stream, the right action of life.

Gifts and sacrifices become routine when they cannot perfect the conscience of the worshiper.[194] Christ's sacrifice is the source of our entering into a right relationship with God. In Him we are called to live a life of sacrifice by a renewal of our mind. It is very evident from

194 Heb 9:9.

what St. Paul says: "I appeal to you therefore, brothers and sisters, by the mercies of God, to present your bodies as a living sacrifice, holy and acceptable to God, which is your spiritual worship" (Rom 12:1)·In other words, it is surrendering our understanding to the all surpassing knowledge of God in faith, and hoping in God when all hopes are found futile and it is always loving because God who is ever present in the soul can preserve and sustain everything for the ultimate good. However, though there is a step of renunciation in everything, yet there will be an inherent joy of being enriched in God as all offerings and sacrifices are channels of grace to make us holy. By this we will be restored from falling into sin and made compensated from imperfections as well.[195]

A new life in Christ with a renewed mind is a way of deepening our union with God and worshipping Him. It is living and offering our entire life with all our faculties as a living sacrifice in faith, hope and love by being holy in Christ to give glory to God.

195 Brian Boyle, "Holiness has a Shape" in *Australian Biblical Review* 2008-09, Vol. 57, 1-21.

Chapter 3

A GLORIOUS AND HOLY TEMPLE IN CHRIST

Introduction

"Those who love me will keep my word, and my Father will love them, and we will come to them and make our home with them" (Jn 14:23). A life that loves Jesus and keeps His word will be freed from all barriers of human structure and will have a life structure formed according to the designs of Jesus who is the way, truth and life. Such souls will be the dwelling place of God and a river (Ezek 47:1-5) in God who is the sea of all power, wisdom, and love. They will fly in God (Is 60:8) and build themselves as glorious and holy temple of God in Christ (Eph 2:21-22). Because, it is in Christ that we are getting perfected in truth and in divine nature and in Christ we receive the fullness of everything. *Christ, however, was faithful over God's house as a son, and we are his house if we hold firm the confidence and the pride that belong to hope* (Heb 3:6). Growing in Christ is growing in this hope. God so loved the world and gave His Only Son not to destroy the world, but to perfect it. Son became the memento of God's love for the world. Growing in Christ is not alienating oneself from the world but enabling us to protect and perfect it in the innocence of its infancy. Only the hope, a sure and steadfast anchor of the soul, a hope that enters the inner shrine behind the curtain (cf. Heb 6:19) alone can enable us to have an innocent faith in the promises of God (Heb 6:14) and live this life with Christ. A life in the outer shrine of senses will not lead us to Christ who sits behind the curtain and a life bound with one's own memory, intellect or will that is the inner shrine in front of the curtain also cannot lead us to Christ. But a transformed mind, a transformed memory, intellect and will in faith, hope and love alone can lead us to this shrine behind the curtain.

In the previous chapters we were dealing how our life is structured and how we are blessed with a structured life with degrees of elevation in Christ, if we follow His word and mind. It is in Christ that a temple of God is perfected by His self-emptying and death on the cross which were the only means of crushing the head of false dignity, and perfecting us. This last chapter will be an analysis of our life structure centred on Christ where our life principles are changed and transformed into divine and how a living temple of God in Christ is formed.

3.1. A Call to be the Living Temple of God

A temple is a place assured with the presence of God or the indwelling of God. Despite many other aspects of the temple it is also a place from where we get infused of this presence of God through grace. The human soul is the dwelling place of God (cf. 1Cor 3:6). And the absence of God in the soul brings in it the feeling of nakedness (Gen 3:7) or shame. It is the presence of God that makes either a place or person the temple of God. Amidst all the aspects of God's presence, our life, or the human face is considered to be the highest expression of God's presence in the world[196] as our life is the replica of His divine power, wisdom and love. Life that lost this presence of God gets renewed in repentance through self-recognition and shame when it feels again this presence (Gen 3: 8; Job 42: 6). Whole creation reminds us of God's presence in its essence; yet, a holy soul without mortal sin is an abiding presence of God in the world through grace,

196 Gregory D'souza, *Contemplative Formation*, (Dhyanavana Publications, Bangalore, 2013) p. 30.

and also a devout soul with an affective presence of Him.[197] In the light of this reflection following aspects are to be considered:

- A temple is a place or a person with the presence of God in essence, grace and affection where no abominations or sin happens.
- Presence of God makes a temple and still more the dwelling of God in human soul who is in likeness and essence sharing God's identity.
- Temple will have its own rituals and so in a living temple, rituals are its living aspects or elements in faith, hope and love.

In the previous chapters we had an analysis, on the centre of human soul that became the top of the mountain where God dwells and how the holy sanctuary of the temple formed the throne and footstool of Yahweh. In the living temple, this throne of God is the centre of the soul where God rests and footstool of Yahweh becomes the lower part of the soul through which God now stays in the world. Here we begin our analysis through a ritual sacrifice which begins at the outer court of our senses through faith and perfecting it with hope in Christ at the interior self and at the 3rd stage as a living sacrifice in love at the centre of the soul where a living temple is formed with God's indwelling.

3.1.1. An Inner Journey with a Sacrificial Offering in the Body

As it is read there was always a custom of purification and it is evident from the sacred Scripture that God cleanses the place that He chooses for his divine purpose. By this fact it can be affirmed that our body with its five sense organs should be cleansed for becoming a living temple and footstool of God by which the act or work of God has to be performed. In the renewed temple there is a sin offering burnt in the outside of sacred area (cf. Ezek 43:21) and at the same time entry into the temple is prohibited to the uncircumcised in heart and flesh (Ezek 44:7). Here there is an emphasis on the purity of heart and

197 John of the Cross, S. C., Stz. 11:3, p. 449.

the body and it is exhorted that body is not a part excluded from the living temple (1Cor 6:19). There is no temple without its rituals. A faith journey to God will begin its initial preparations in the body itself with a little sacrifices and mortifications of humble steps like a one cubit measure the prophet could find (Ezek 40: 5-8). The means to these steps of sacrifice will be surely the three theological virtues, the true channels with sacramental grace that can attune our whole self to Christ. Any soul with true faith can receive all the promised merits of this living sacrifice (Heb. 11) of Christ. As the love of God in us generates and progress from the Holy Trinity, this love passes through three stages of formation, i.e., knowing God, experiencing God and flowering out with Charisma.

In this first stage of progress in the inner journey towards God, our desire to get prepared or equipped within ourselves will prompt us to get deprived of all worldly pleasures. In this stage not only the desire alone will help us to get departed from them but anything we do in faith as the preparation for this departure will have its own value before God. Interior penances and conversion accomplished in daily life from the source of Holy Eucharist and acts of reconciliation[198] will confirm and strengthen one in faith, hope and love. In short, liberation through faith means a liberation and protection through prayer by accepting the events of daily life from the liberating and protecting hand of God with wisdom, understanding and knowledge. For, our struggle is not against enemies of flesh and blood or it is not merely from mere human beings who are our brethren, but against the spiritual forces of evil in the heavenly places (cf. Eph 6:12). The protecting wall around the temple surroundings indicates this protection through prayer.

3.1.2. The Stages of Elevation to Holiness[199]

For the one who is in journey it is necessary to know from where he started? to where he goes? and where he is now? This awareness makes his journey easy and peaceful. The journey of Prophet Ezekiel

---

198 C. C.C.#. 1430-1433, pp. 399-400.

199 Mary O' Driscoll (ed.) *Catherine of Siena; Passion for the Truth Compassion for Humanity* (New City Press, New York, 1993) pp. 107-111.

was an upward journey, yet there was an aspect of getting deepened in holiness through humility as it progressed high to the mountain top. It was a journey to the sanctuary of God. Similar is the in-word journey that John of the Cross explains in his structural analysis of human soul. As the spiritual journey progresses, there is an in-depth digging and rooting of oneself in detachment through wisdom and extolling oneself through attachment to Christ. This growth in wisdom is the recognition of one's nothingness as well as the richness of God's glory and holiness that deepens in real humility. The yield of this up-word but in-word journey is a clear vision of God with three different but progressive stages of genuine conversion, progress and experience.[200] Here at the first level of humility and self-abnegation, one gets into the grace to grow in ankle deep and is able to kiss at the feet of Christ. This love will enable one to be the faithful servant of God (cf. Jn 13:16-17). Here the soul will be able to climb the steps of outer court of senses to the inner court of interior faculties with a progress in divine knowledge.

How much deep the root, the tree will be safer to grow higher. A bit more growth in humility through negation of selfish love will take one to fix in knee deep and up to the waist. This degree of love will extol the soul to be the friend of Jesus (cf. Jn 15:14-15) and is able to kiss at His hand. Life through an inner disciplining of self and the formation of interior faculties by getting attuned with the mind of Christ will enable the soul to pass the inner court of the living temple up to the vestibule of the temple proper.

A deep journey further to God through the divine wisdom will enable the soul to get into a perfect union of the will and gets the kiss of His cheek. Here God's will be soul's will (cf. Lk 1:38; 22:42). This degree of love can be compared either of a filial love or the bridal love.[201] In this stage, the soul runs swiftly and gently into the holy of holies or to the deepest centre where the life is ruled by the divine wisdom or conscience of one's own soul where the Holy Trinity indwells. The following part will be an analysis of the

---

200 Egan D. Harvey, *An Anthology of Christian Mysticism*, (The Liturgical Press, Minnesota, 1996) p. 169.

201 Allen–Johan Bergstrom (ed.), *Climbing the Mountain, The Carmelite Journey*, (Saint Albert's Press & Edizioni Carmelitane, U K, 2010) p. 207.

growth processes symbolized as an inward journey to the living temple through three stages: liberation, confirmation and restoration (1Pt.5:6-11) just as one passes the outer court, inner court and the temple proper.

3.1.2.1. Liberation from the Sensual World at the Outer Court

The first and the preliminary condition of a holy temple is the faith aspect of the assurance of divine presence and divine act in a place that is holy and made consecrated for the same purpose. Liberation through faith includes: faith in God's hand or grace that liberates a soul that is drowned in the imperfections and impossibilities of this life. And a living temple is the visible body of a human being consecrated to God for the divine purpose. The soul that desires to become such temple of God gets into this initial convictions and very intimate knowledge of God with one's own unique experiences. This is a stage in which a soul gets into the initial convictions and very intimate knowledge of God with one's own unique experiences. This initial experience makes the soul to fall or prostrate before God with true reverence, repentance and fear (cf. Ezek 1:28)· It is the Hand of God that liberates a soul that is drowned in the imperfections, and impossibilities of this life. But, only what God demand from us in the beginning is that we should grow in our faith in Him. Because our faith alone is that pleases God. Winds against our faith may cause again to fall, yet learning to get up and stand firm in faith is necessary. This is a grace that affirms the soul in faith to begin the journey. This will be a growth journey by climbing the seven steps, the gifts of the Holy Spirit: wisdom, understanding, knowledge, counsel, fortitude, piety, fear of God and this fear of God with the acknowledgement of His supremacy is the beginning of all wisdom.

The visibility and presence of anything or anyone is naturally presented and possible through its outer part. Our body with its five sense organs are the outer part that presents us in the world. Preserving it for its real goal is our aim. Any seed with its outer shell or flesh is for the protection and growth of the real nut in it. As we discussed in the previous chapters, our body the lower part of the soul protects and nourishes our soul with similar duty. Following part is an analysis of this process of protecting and nourishing our souls by accepting oneself in and through Christ - the real temple.

i. Accepting and Loving Oneself

There is no greater love than sacrificing one's life for the sake of the other. Yet, love can be defined according to the context of the recipient or actor. Sinners also love as they are loved. Therefore, instead of defining love in many words, in general it can be called as energy. This energy can be positive or negative. This positive energy is God and the power of God is the power of love. God's love is defined in terms of self-sacrifice or giving Himself through His Beloved Son for the sake of the world (cf. Jn 3:17). God's love is always productive, dynamic and at work. As God is everlasting, His love never ends, but remains in one or the other form or it transforms. Though love seems to be an emotion or passion in form, the engine behind is the energy that causes someone or something to move into the object loved.[202] After the true knowledge and experience of God, at the end the journey of flowering begins within oneself. Without getting armed or assured of one's own safety, no one can start a journey to save the other. Without accepting or loving oneself, we can never accept or love the other in perfect charity. Hence, all our initial sacrifices of sin offered at the outside of the sacred area or in other words in the exterior senses of our self can be offered for one's own salvation.

ii. Holiness: The Enclosure Wall to Safeguard the Temple Surroundings

After getting departed from the outer court; the sensuality, the enclosure wall is made by safeguarding the lower sensory parts such as the memory, phantasy and imagination from distractions and everything that deprives of its inner peace. It is remembering from what one has fallen and with a repentance, remaining back to the initial grace and an awareness of the distractions and temptations of evil without allowing them to rule over the interior self. In order to make ourselves a holy temple, the lower part of the soul; i.e., the five sense organs with our fantasy and imagination should be protected

---

202 Francis De Sales, Vincent Kerins, (tr.), *The Love of God*, (S. F. S. Publications, Asian Trading Corporation, Bangalore, 1982) p. 16.

always with a conviction of divine presence and remembrance. Constant invoking of God's presence and help along with little acts of devotions accustomed and practiced by the traditions of the holy Church in availing the indulgences also will be the manner of acquiring this safety and protection. In the Temple vision the temple area is surrounded with an enclosure wall. "Now there was a wall all around the outside of the temple area" (Ezek 40:5). At first the enclosure wall around the sacred area, is measured. The wall around the temple area can emphasize the need to safeguard the enclosed space.[203] This wall will take us to launch the spiritual journey with which the prophet himself began his prophetic call: "and put siege works against it, and build a siege wall against it, and cast up a ramp against it; set camps also against it, and plant battering rams against it all around" (Ezek 4:2). This part will take us through a realization of everything that is against a soul that travels towards God who is Holy. Divine power that flows through prayer and life of holiness is the protecting wall that resists the entry of profane. The only height measurement given[204] here can stand for the heavenly protection the soul gains before the journey in its initial operations. If the boundaries are protected well with the divine guards, the safety of the temple is assured.

It is in this connection one has to see the journey described by John of the Cross. He begins his journey of ascend with a departure or escape. This departure or escape helps the soul to live without encumbrance from anything else. According to him, this is a privation and purgation from all sensible appetites through a holy and devoted life and an attraction by God enkindled with love. By the words "not touch the wall"[205] and "by the wall" John of the Cross refers to the enclosure of peace and the fence of virtues and perfections by which the soul is shut in and protected, because, the soul is the garden

203 Brian Boyle, "'Holiness has a Shape: The Place of the Altar in Ezekiel's Visionary Plan of Sacral Space (Ez 43:1-12, 13-17, 18-27)", *Australian Biblical Review* 2008-09) Vol. 57, pp. 1-21.

204 Joseph Blenkinsopp, *Interpretation, A Bible Commentary for Teaching and Preaching*, pp. 201-239.

205 John of the Cross, S. C. stz. 21:18, p. 495.

which is enclosed and protected solely for the Beloved, and among whose flowers He browses.

By departing from the joy, affections and movements of the sensory world, the safety measure is kept for the outskirts: the lower sensory parts such as the memory, phantasy and imagination as they are the districts outside the walls of the city. For John city is the innermost part, or the threshold of the soul which is capable of communion with God[206] where God – is – there (Ezek 48:35). By keeping away from the distractions and everything that deprives of its inner peace the soul is made quiet in prayer and the enclosure wall is made. Here there the soul is always obliged to make a process of renewal to remain in the innocence of initial grace or the initial experiences of divine call. It is remembering from where one has fallen and with repentance continuously remains back to the initial grace.

This is also an awareness of the distractions and temptations of evil and not allowing them to rule over the interior self from the beginning itself. The wall around the temple area can emphasize the firm mind or the assurance, the soul preserves amidst all its affliction, poverty and slander that can come from any side. For the soul it is a protecting wall for the purification and purgation. These will have an end and the soul will be able to take them as momentary compared to the life in purgatory just as the prophet took the symbolic days one day for one year. Thus, the soul in this process will be accepting them all as part of the journey to become a holy temple and the city where God dwells.

By this awareness of a protecting wall that everything is for the safety of the journey, the soul gets free from fear and grows in courage that will enable the soul to gain the crown at the end. Here, so many things may happen around, but the soul in sojourn will not be lost of her faith and learns to repent and pray for all those who are suffering the same. By this the soul will be able to reach the city with an escort of her beloveds (cf. Esth 7:3-5).

For keeping oneself not being exhausted of grace and the oil of virtues, the soul is ready to protect oneself by the wall of disguised

---

206 John of the Cross, S. C. stz. 18:8, p. 485.

form in faith, hope and love in order to work and live more for the sake of God's name. Here the soul is not ready to show even any compassion towards one's own weaknesses and desires to live more and more for the sake of God's name and considers comparing to the life in purgatory, reaching perfection by suffering and living with God in this world itself as the strong walls of protection. Even to the last moment of her life, the soul feels the need of repentance and remains in submission to the power and grace of God through His mercy. Therefore, the mercy and grace of God also becomes a protecting wall.

iii. 'Departure' in Application with Faith

When love takes root, it always makes the inward and outward exercise of love in order to resemble the Beloved and share the beauty. For climbing the mountain is growing in the knowledge and experience of the divine Word the Son of God in faith. After the climbing of this mountain the soul does not remain quiet there but leaps down to the hills and valleys. It means, the perfect knowledge and wisdom of Christ enables persons to understand and comprehend the treasures of divine works and mysteries in other creatures and realities found in the whole cosmos. This wisdom leads the soul to leap down and up through the 10 steps of mystical ladder[207] according to the loving need and desires that the Holy Spirit instil in her. Hence, the soul travels through the mountains, hills and valleys.[208] As the effect of a life consecrated in faith, an initial step of a sacrificial life of love with an attempt for the reparation of our sins takes place. A life and all its activities with a self-examination of conscience with regard to seven cardinal sins and commandments of God at the altar of our soul will enable us to complete the sin offering (cf. Ezek 43:25-27). The saints who found even the smallest actions with great love brought forth abundant fruit they intended.[209]

---

207 John of the Cross, D. N., II. Chs. 19, 20, p. 373.

208 John of the Cross, S. C. stz. 36, p. 547-8.

209 Allen–Johan Bergstrom (ed.), *Teresa of Jesus' Climbing the Mountain, The Carmelite Journey*, (Saint Albert's Press & Edizioni Carmelitne, United Kingdom, 2010), p. 302.

- The symbolic days the prophet took one day for one year (Ezek. 4:6) in his initial preparations can be applicable for a believer when we begin our spiritual journey with spirit of penance and mortifications with the intention of one's own holiness.
- The friends of Job who found the intensity of his sufferings as great spent with him seven days and nights in silence with him (Job 2:13). Here lies the relevance of mediation of the other in prayer. Every little action and attitude has a meaning and it becomes the channels of grace for the soul who hold faith in God.
- By faith the walls of Jericho fell after they had been encircled for seven days (cf. Heb. 11:30). Any act of devotion with the pure intention of beseeching God's protection will save a soul who has only God as refuge.
- Saul waiting in Gilgal seven days, the time appointed by Samuel (1 Sam. 13:8).

All these were the acts of prayer in faith that transformed their life into an indwelling experience of God where God worked and they surrendered. The same is the way prescribed for anyone who wish to take the journey of faith to the inner mount.

iv. Distinguishing the Touch of God in the Winds of Life

Winds represent the natural or unexpected events of life. As it is mentioned in the previous chapters, each wind has its own effect in life. Either destructive or constructive; they speak to us something. Learning from them for the life left before us is a good sign (cf. Lk. 12:54-59). In the beginning of the divine vision, the Prophet Ezekiel faced a north wind (Ezek 1:4). Job could hear Yahweh from the heart of the tempest (Job 38:1; 40:6). After the entire hurricane, earthquake, fire, and a sheer silence prophet Elijah could hear God from a murmuring sound (1King 19:11-13).

For a believer, nothing in life is meaningless, waist or useless. Everything in life, whether accidental or intended has a purpose for God, and they will effect in us according to our receptivity. One way or the other they will be causing good results either for us or for others through us. Hence having a positive and a mystical outlook on all the storms and winds of life can design our life with a transforming vision. It is just like the understanding of God a soul has in the beginning of the purgative stages and later when the enlightenment happens how the soul feels of God. In short, our life structure is designed according to our theory or the measuring reed, with which we measure our life experiences or on what we build our living temple. Faith in the Cross of Christ liberates, restores and affirms the soul to begin the journey.

Though the term "soul" refers to the innermost aspect of man, often it refers the entire human person that is intended to become, in the body of Christ, a holy temple of the Spirit.[210] Hence, we are invariably obliged to keep our body purified and holy in God. Our actions, talk, look, and inclinations or feelings, taste and sense also must be supportive and leading to this goal. There is no temple that encourages marketing where sacrifices and worships are supposed to be done (Jn 2:14-16).

3.1.2.2. Confirmation at the Inner Court – at the Interior Faculties through Hope

The aspect of holiness is confirmed in the temple along with its holy vessels. The relevance of holy vessels affirms the punishments given to the king Belshazzar: "You have exalted yourself against the Lord of heaven! The vessels of his temple have been brought in before you, and you and your lords, your wives and your concubines have been drinking wine from them" (Dan 5:23-28). Our interior faculties are these vessels that use to perform the task of sacrifices and offerings. The food and medicine for these interior faculties are the wisdom, understanding and knowledge. The Word of God that is made flesh through Jesus cleanses our interior faculties and these vessels become holy in the living temple. After a stage of liberation and purification at the external senses through faith, the journey proceeds to the interior faculties to confirm this faith with hope and performs the task of sacrifices for further sanctification in a deeper level.

210 C.C.C. #. 364, p. 104.

The journey to the inmost centre of the soul which John of the Cross deals with and the journey to the renewed temple of God which the Prophet Ezekiel explains both are a journey that is of inward in nature. As the journey proceeds, the passageway widened from story to story; because the structure is supplied with offsets: the faith, hope and love which widens as life proceeds - all around the wall of the temple to serve as supports (cf. Ezek. 41:6-7). The faith in which we get rooted in the beginning will enable us to stand firm in hope (cf. Ezek. 2:1; 1 Pt. 5:9). It is our readiness to take the spiritual journey always as a beginning. It is a call to a pilgrimage that has to be steadfast. The faith will help us to get strengthened in hope and we will begin to accept and love our own self from the hand of God.

Here the soul in sojourn of liberation or restoration enters into a second stage that is of confirmation. "The one who has hope lives differently: the one who hopes has been granted the gift of a new life."[211] It is 'hope' that makes our life different and it will be always a hope centred on the best of than what we hold now. Growth in hope is a growth in the redemptive love of Christ. It is a journey towards the assurances of life that is promised in Christ. Our hope is not rooted in the goodness that we hold but in the sacrificial and redemptive love of God that is granted to us through His Beloved Son Jesus (cf. 1Jn 4:10). But Just like the beatitudes (Mt 5:1-12), the promises of Christ is obtainable only after a stage of purgation and illumination by the flashing light (cf. Ezek. 1:13) and cautery[212] and it begins in the house hold of God (1Pt. 4:17) where He makes His dwelling.

God makes his dwelling with the one who holds nothing as his own and also who possess a clean and pure heart. The way to attain this stage is submitting our intellect to God by faith, and fixing our memory in Christ to have a constant evaluation and identification of our life with Him. It is also allowing our will and strength to be directed by the power and Spirit of God through Christ. The more we free ourselves from the exterior aspects and structures

---

211 Benedict XVI, *Spe Salvi*, (Encyclical Letter on Christian Hope, 30th November 2007), (Libreria Editrice Vaticana, Vatican, 2007) p. 6.

212 John of the Cross, L. F. stz. 2, p. 596.

and concentrate on the interior clarity, the better we succeed in simplifying our spiritual life in love and wisdom, and the more our union with God becomes a reality.[213] The more we grow in wisdom through Christ, the deeper we possess the hope that enables the will to be united with God and to the eternal rewards. This hope will calm our interior self and strengthen us to discard the profits of the present in order to hold the best from the Hands of God and possess a balanced mind with Christ in every ups and downs of life. The wisdom that comes from Christ will build the interior peace and make every yoke easy and burden light for a suffering soul (Mt 11:30).

3.1.2.2.1. Christ –the Way to Wisdom[214]

For John of the Cross, union with God is consummating the intellect with God's wisdom and will with His love.[215] In the Letter to the Romans St. Paul puts forward a question "For who has known the mind of the Lord?" (Rom 11:34). One could say that Jesus already has given answer for this question with full conviction. By the saying in the Gospel of John "Righteous Father, the world does not know you, but I know you" (Jn. 17:25) Jesus make us convinced that He knows the mind of God. Though God's mind is hidden to us, mind of Christ whose mind is a visible mind of God, is revealed to us. Hence, knowing Christ's mind is the perfection of knowledge. For in him all the fullness of God was pleased to dwell (cf. Col 1:19). Purity of a person depends also on the purity of the mind and this truth is affirmed by the statement of Jesus that "You have already been cleansed by the word that I have spoken to you" (Jn. 15:3). The following parts of this chapter will be an analysis of the knowledge God profuse to the intellect and how the soul is able to travel through an illuminative way with the support of a lighted candle who is Christ.

---

213 Carlo Carretto, Sarah Fawcett, (tr.), In Search of the Beyond, (Daughters of St. Paul, Bombay, 1976) pp. 110-111.

214 Bar 3:35-37.

215 John of the Cross, S C. stz. 39:14-15, pp. 562-3.

i. Intellect –An Island to Know God[216]

The following analysis on the inner court or the interior faculties of the soul will give a vivid picture of this way of ascend to the mountain of perfection. As the spiritual journey proceeds, the soul finds everything in the world as temporary and learns to count them as only means to climb the mountain of perfection. Finding the mystical dimension of everything in the world, the soul learns to withdraw oneself from every aspect of its busy involvement and gives much importance to the eternal realities and works for them more. This growth in the wisdom and knowledge helps the intellect to separate the person and invest all his energies into a marvellous island of heavenly riches and treasures. Compared with other men he is withdrawn from people and is singular and superior in his deeds and works to achieve this strange knowledge. Here the soul also finds a God who is very strange, unique, marvellous and wonderful in loving her so personally, and being with her as if the only one loved by Him with an unfathomable mercy and compassion. His ways, counsels, and works are very peculiar, new and wonderful to the soul here.

Here the spiritual knowledge that the intellect receives are far-off to all the senses and also to natural knowledge. Hence, the intellect becomes a strange island. By quoting the verse from the book of Job "I had heard of you by the hearing of the ear, but now my eye sees you" (Job 42:5) John of the Cross explains how the intellect becomes the unique receptor of divine knowledge even without any help of the other senses in hearing and seeing God.

We are taught by the mystical wisdom[217] that comes through the anointing we received from the Holy Spirit who abides in us (cf. 1Jn 2:27). This is the teaching of the Holy Spirit that Jesus promised; "But the Advocate, the Holy Spirit, whom the Father will send in my name, will teach you everything, and remind you of all that I have said to you" (Jn 14:26). There was a time where fathers were holy yet, there sons went astray (1 Sam 3:11-14; 8:1-5) and now, even if

---

216 John of the Cross, S .C. stzs. 14 & 15: 8-21, pp. 464-471.

217 Cf. Gregory D'souza, *Mystical Wisdom*, (Dhyanavana Publications, Bangalore, 2016) pp. 75-76.

the fathers are sinners the Holy Spirit whom the Father has sent in the name of Jesus will make the children holy (Ezek 18:1-20).

Intellect now learns from the divine knowledge in which it was ignorant earlier, and it now begins to affirm its faith through resisting struggle and detaching from everything that does not please God, practices every virtue that helps to possess Christ, and wait in hope with readiness to infill God's wisdom that takes to a direct contact with the mystery of God. The soul now perfects life by becoming more of synthesis by going beyond oneself and entering into a life transformed with more humility that includes the other and God.[218]

Now at this stage of confirmation; everything that we received in faith will be able to live and affirm with hope. For the attainment of so high state of perfection or ascend to the high mountain, the lower part should be surrendered and made subject to the higher part, and also it is necessary to attain an adequate degree of purity, fortitude and love. It implies that a stepping forward with a good moral life and the practice of virtue which are necessary for a life of holiness and growth in the contemplative wisdom.

ii. A Memory that Rests in God

Often the major part of our life is lived in the past and we are turned back from the right reason and travels back from the real goal. We forget to live in the present or our memory carries us away from the present without even our awareness or consent. The five sense organs along with the reduced inner faculties; the fantasy and the imagination may always distract the memory to the world which is tangible and visible to them. But, a clear intellect brings a clean reflection of the memory. An intellect that found God within oneself is a hook or peg that control or regulate the memory to the right direction. It is in our memory that all that we have eaten with the intellect get chewed and digested well. As the outcome of a good and right intellect the reflection that arises touches the good decisions and principles that come from the will.

When all the chaos of the world withdraws from our memory, there get a chance for the wisdom of God to takes birth in us. Jesus

218 Cf. Gregory D'souza, *Mystical Wisdom*, pp. 80-84.

identifies Himself with a physician of our soul by saying that "Those who are well have no need of a physician, but those who are sick; I have come to call not the righteous but sinners" (cf. Mk 2:17). Only in the redeeming power of Christ the crucified, and in His gentle and humble Heart (cf. Mt 11:29), our wounded and disturbed memories get rest. Memory is considered as a possessive faculty where the impressions of our experiences are stored.[219] A memory that learns everything from Christ possesses and relishes all the tranquillity, rest and quietude of the peaceful night and obscure divine knowledge.[220] Memory takes the position of covering wings that touches both ends one at the edge of the intellect and other connecting with the will just as the wings of hope supports and affirms the faith and enables love to be established with a new strength at the will. The soul at this stage of growth learns to concentrate the memories on Christ and relishes life in divine wisdom. Such souls will experience the movement of the Spirit of God amidst all the chaos off waters and destructive winds of life. Concentrating our reflection to God in itself is forming us to be the temple of God. And a grain offering of gratitude through Christ to the Heavenly Father will be the best and favourable offering that can be lived at this place of our interior faculty.

iii. Will with Hope-at the Altar of Sacrifice on the Way to the Ascend

Rebellion is no less a sin than divination, and stubbornness is like iniquity and idolatry (1 Sam. 15:23). The word of God says that: "elders and dignitaries are the head, and prophets who teach lies are the tail" (Isa 9:15). Just like Samuel hewed Agag in pieces before the Lord in Gilgal (cf. 1Sam 15:33), the head of false dignity was crushed in Golgotha (cf. Mt 27:33) with the crucifixion of Christ there. Now everyone who is poisoned with the false dignity is healed when they look at the face of the Crucified Christ and is filled with real humility in which we learn to be a child not an elder (cf. Mt 18:3-5). Yet the process of reaching this stage is an act of getting sacrificed within at the altar of the will. Will is a power or activity proper to the soul as

219 Gregory D'souza, *Contemplative Formation*, p. 15.

220 John of the Cross, S. C. stz. 14 & 15:22, p. 471.

principle. Here, knowledge received through the faculties becomes acknowledgements and accordingly decision takes place with a new value or principle by the will and are distinctively transferred into the body with spontaneous actions and thus the soul enters into the acts of hope that produces eternal rewards and abiding grace.[221] A Will that is united with God in hope becomes ready to get sacrificed of everything that is not God. "It seems to me that I have found my heaven on earth since heaven is God and God is in my soul"[222] says blessed Elizabeth of the Trinity. Such convictions in life will make many altars within one's self where sacrifices with true love, repentance and gratitude take place.

a) *Sacrifice of love:* The soul here recognizes the strength and weakness with which God has adorned her and acknowledges the divine love that God poured on her through Christ. Here, what matters is not the measure of goodness or love that the soul has towards God, but the love that God has for the soul, disregarding all its infirmities. With the conviction of this love, the soul finds within many occasions of sacrificing love for God. It is the untiring love with which the soul lives for the sake of God's Name (cf. Rev 2:3).
b) *Sacrifice of repentance:* It is the growing attitude of acknowledging one's sinfulness and accepting everything in life with an attitude of repentance and reparation. It is an expression of the inability of soul by itself growing advanced in God's love, but only at the mercy of God. It is a constant process of growing in humility (cf. Rev 2:4-5; 3:17-19).
c) *Sacrifice of gratitude:* The growing gratitude towards God who loves her with an unconditional love enables soul to withstand all the sufferings and test by obeying and keeping the word of God (cf. Rev 3:8, 10). This gratitude also helps the soul to depart from the sensual world in love whenever it requires for the union of the will with God.

221 Antonio Rosmini, *Development of the Human Soul*, Denis Cleary, Watson Terence (tr.), Rosmini House, Durham, 1989) Vol. 2, p. 167.

222 Allen–Johan Bergstrom, (ed.), *"Teresa of Jesus" Climbing the Mountain, The Carmelite Journey*, p. 207.

This sacrificial offering is an emphasis on the relevance of becoming holy. Slight sacrifices and mortifications practiced in the divine name is the ritual sacrifices intended. This growth in the faculty of will as a sacrificial offering prepares the soul to be a lovelier dwelling place of God. This is a call from God to all who are gifted with life. A transformation in the knowledge and understanding in the realm of these faculties can form us to accept the Hands of God that comes to us in various forms as a token of perfection. Preparing the above said sacrifices in ascend to mount of self is quiet enough to build such living temples.

3.1.2.3. Restoration through Love – from the Temple Proper

This is a stage where the soul reaches to love God by leaping ups and downs through the 10 steps of mystical ladder. It is a life that is restored in a perfect and purified love in relation with oneself, others and God. When Moses wanted to go across to look the blazing but not being burnt up bush, God said to him, "Come no closer! Remove the sandals from your feet, for the place on which you are standing is holy ground" (Ex 3:2-5). This anxiety and freedom in our own life towards the impossibilities may happen when God works through us. While God works through our soul, we are taught, not to take the authorship or the freedom over it, but to stand in awe and count our own self a holy place that God uses for His purpose and to leave it for Him alone. When God uses, it burns for Him and only for the glory of God, it can never be burnt up, but will be ever green.

In the midst of this action of God there is a human part with an activating grace where we need to be ready to remove or avoid turning back to take our sandals that stands for our own safety or enjoyment of its fruits. Accepting this life of grace as the real path or the way of life is according to one's need and sufficiency of the nourishments available in it and also how it matters in glorifying God. Word of God waters the soil according to the Supreme Will of the Father. In the further call of Moses, he was appointed with a mission of saving the souls who were in slavery. The fruit of this mission was after redeeming themselves; they all together were able to worship God, who dwelt within their soul and worked miraculously from the mountain top of their interior self. And they could recognize the work of God's hand that saved them by His power than sword (cf. Josh 10:11). Here, soul is restored and established in divine love that prepares oneself to live for the glory of God's Name to any extent as the spirit of God wishes and also to live for the other as God desires. Such souls begin their journey from the temple proper that is the submission of their will at the altar of Christ who taught the beauty and value of true submission.

3.1.2.3.1. Dining with Christ (at the East Gate of Life)

Christ who stands at the east gate of our life with its full authority is the sacrificial beast standing at the door post (cf. Heb. 13:12; Jn. 19:13, 37) of our interior faculties where he is being crucified at our every sin. Christ is the real guide and perfect model for forming and maintaining us as a living temple. As a faithful servant of the house of God at every need Christ surrendered the lower part of His soul to the Father in heaven by lifting His hands and eyes to the Almighty God praising and thanking Him aloud at every prayer in need. He became an eternal priest, offering himself as a sacrifice for us by the offering of his interior faculties; the total submission of his self in order to transform all the winds of our life. At the end, he commended also his Spirit into the hands of the heavenly Father. As our souls are of God's possession, the Holy Spirit, the wind from Christ is able to bring shame on all who does abominations on the altar of self, as our sins pierce and wounds the humble and gentle Heart of Christ (cf. Jn. 19:37; Rev 1:7). "A wind has wrapped them in its wings, and they shall be ashamed because of their altars" (Hos. 4:19). And it is the repentant heart that recognizes the bridegroom of the soul and will mourn for Him; as one mourns for an only child, and weeps bitterly over him; as one weeps over a firstborn (cf. Zech. 12:10). The rebuke of God is not with a rod, but with true atonement and this repentance will carry away all the east wind of falsehood and violence that we hear and pursues all day long (Hos. 12:1). The grace of discernment our intellect and memory get with faith, hope and love will win now these evils and the wind of the Holy Spirit will wipe them away, as the tempest or the Pentecost of the Holy Spirit scatters them and makes us to rejoice and glory in the Lord alone. In Christ and in the wings of His Spirit alone can we find again, unite and reconcile the lost ones and broken relations (cf. Is 41:16; 59:19; 43:5). These escorts are the consolation, by the prophets of God promised to a soul who is ready to suffer for the salvation of one's own soul and the souls of others (cf. Ezek 14:22; Is. 43:5; Bar. 5:6).

3.1.2.3.2 Golgotha with the Role of Gilgal

In their journey to the Promised Land, Gilgal was an important place for the Israelites. They encamped there, it was a place for them to begin and return (cf. Josh 10:6-7, 9, 15, 43), a place for anointment, offering their sacrifices, (cf. 1 Sam 10:1, 8; 11:14-15), defeated and killed the enemies and made treaties there (cf. 1Sam 15:33, Josh 9:6; 10:6) and also was a place to meet the king, (cf. 1 Sam 13:4; 2 Sam 19:15), a starting place for Angel of the Lord (cf. Jud 2:1), a place of allotment of properties for the tribes of Judah, (cf. Josh 14:6), and a place made holy by God (cf. Josh 5:9-10, 15). However, Gilgal became a place at where the disgraces are rolled away. "Today I have rolled away from you the disgrace of Egypt." And so that place is called Gilgal to this day.

Now, for the new Israel, the place to meet all the events mentioned above is only the altar of Christ where the living moments of Golgotha are taken place and where all the disgraces of slavery of sin is rolled away and the souls are able to get anointed by the Holy Spirit to a life of royal priesthood. In the divine light, our eyes from the window behind the wall of interior faculties are able to gaze everything with a clear vision. The understanding that the Holy Spirit gives us will lead us to the deepest centre of the self where all the enemies of the soul are annihilated including the last but the strongest one as Samuel killed Agag in Gilgal. This vision of the inner eye will enable us to pray for the persecutors and experience the strength and light so that one may find protection under the suffering and find favour of those who persecute us. It means, the transformation of those who cause suffering for us (cf. Bar 1:11-12). The obedience to these suffering circumstances is the condition of possessing the Promised Land (Bar 2:21). Repentance towards the failure of keeping this command is reflected in the attitude of the exiles (Bar 2:24). The life of Christ was the affirmation of this conviction and in order to win the sinners, he drunk to the dregs the bowl of wrath. However, by perfecting the suffering He made it salvific and built an eternal living temple in which we all form to be a temple in Christ: "O Israel, how great is the house of God, how vast the territory that he possesses!" (Bar 3:24). The Humble and gentle Heart of Christ has no boundary in accepting all; the sinners and saints. "It is great and has no bounds; it is high and immeasurable" (Bar 3:25).

As it is with everyone, Christ also made a deed in distributing His properties. Though his properties were invisible at that moment, it was formed from the right beginning of His invisibility as "in Memory of Him." Now even if the experience of Christ is beyond the place, time, and persons according to the faith one holds; for knowing Christ, the authentic and possible channel is only the Church and its sacramental territories and authorities appointed by Christ. The only true channel of grace that flows from the life-giving temple is the Altar of His sacrifice. The features and relevance of the Altar of Christ is very important in the life of a believer in reaching to the perfection required for the entry of the promised land-the heaven, as the features or the relevance of Gilgal in the life of Israelites in entering to the promised land, the Canaan.

The following elements and features of the Altar of Christ are based on the aspects of Gilgal as mentioned above.

i. A place to begin and return: Just as Joshua established the twelve stones brought from Jordan (Josh 4:20), the Church of Christ is established and built upon the foundation of the twelve apostles and prophets, with Christ Jesus himself as the cornerstone (cf. Eph. 2:20). After their journey through desert, it was in Gilgal that the chosen ones of Israel could do their circumcision and celebrate the Passover (cf. Jos. 5:10-11) and from there onwards they could begin to eat what the land produced, the unleavened bread and roasted ears of corn. And it was from Gilgal they began all their journey of attack in conquering their enemies and returned to this camp for rest and refreshments.

For every new beginning it is the altar of Christ which stands in memory of Golgotha which is our morning sacrifice that gives life, strength, guidance and light. This is the perfect place where we can put all our applications and supplications to God, as our prayer before a task. After all the tiresome works, it is only the Altar of Christ that gives us rest, consolation, refreshments and renewing life that we get. And it is the altar of Christ where we can offer our thanks in the best and greatest form after all our gains and losses. Just as the circumcision, it is here that we can receive the grace of circumcising our hearts through the sacrament of reconciliation and can have our pass over meal.

ii. A place for anointment, offer sacrifices: The official place of anointment for the Israelites as they requested for a king was the Gilgal. It is here that Saul was anointed by Samuel as the king for Israelites. It is the altar of Christ, the only source, for the new Israel, the church finds as the holy place for all the anointments. The only place for offering sacrifices to God also is this moving Golgotha.

iii. A place to defeat and kill the enemies and make treaties: Just as Samuel killed the enemy Agag in Gilgal and Gibeonites made treaty with Joshua, it is at the altar of Christ that the spirit of enmity is eradicated and we get freedom from all the bondages and slavery of evil. And it is in the merit of Christ's sacrifice that we get the grace for the reconciliation and are able to accept everyone as part of accepting our brethren in God, with a spirit of reconciliation and reunion where all the broken relations are restored.

iv. A place to meet the king: Christ Jesus is our king and prince of our souls. And only assured and anointed place where we can receive Him with the majesty of heaven and dine with Him as the Manna of our souls is the Altar of Christ. A king is the protector, provider, and ruler. Christ the king who comes to meet us every day at His table is a faithful ruler who guarantees our safety, comfort and surety. And his rules are very light and easy that He writes it with a unique love into our hearts and minds.

v. A starting place for Angel of the Lord: It is from the altar of God that each one gets the message for themselves from the messengers of God. The angels of God acts and reacts for the chosen ones; right from the altar to the place at where their daily life influences and with which they are surrounded.

vi. A place for allotment of properties: As part of conquering and living in the promised land, Joshua distributes each part of the land for all the tribes of Israel according to their need. And just as the sons of Judah met Joshua in Gilgal, the children of Christ, meet Him at His table of sacrifice for their needs and He surely provides them according to their requirement and no one is left from there with an empty hand.

vii. A place made holy by God: It is the altar of Christ, the moving Golgotha that makes the whole church holy. Where ever this memory of Golgotha takes place, there the holy church is formed and all the disgraces of persons and even such places are taken away. It was in Gilgal that the Israelites had their pass over meal after their long journey through the deserts; this pass over was a foretaste of the culmination of that which is going to be fulfilled in Jehoshua – the Son of God, who would take us to the eternity of promised heaven. He liberates us from slavery of sin to the salvation through the events of Golgotha.

It is only Jesus who claimed of himself as the temple of God by saying: "Destroy this temple, and in three days I will raise it up" (Jn. 2:19). And only from His temple sanctuary flows the streams of living water. And those who are budded in Him will produce the same effect. One may begin the spiritual journey with very glorious experiences of God as the Prophet Ezekiel experienced with his divine vision in Chebar; but at the end the soul reaches to an experience of God's holiness with nothing as his/her requirements just as Job experienced in his theophany (Job. 42:5-6) and Ezekiel who found the throne of God at the end in the temple vision not even with a human form in contrast to all his glorious experiences of previous visions. This experience of nothingness can be possessed only at the perfect realization of the Sacrifice at Golgotha.

3.1.2.3.3. Holiness from the Holy of Holies

For the reception of natural or supernatural wisdom, one needs holiness. Holiness from Holy Eucharist is an invitation to be a renewed temple in Christ. What has to be renewed is one's own ruined life. The Holy Spirit of God who restored the crucified Christ from the tomb will renew our dead self from the tomb of sinful world. The life-giving water that flows from the altar of Christ is the grace of the Holy Spirit. One who learns to do this inward journey will possess the indwelling of the Holy Trinity from the table of the sacrificial lamb. They will be able to read their own life scroll not with anyone but only with Christ-the sacrificial lamb (Rev 5). Anyone who read his or her life along with a Christ experience will never find anything cursed in him or her but even the negative experiences of life will be a fertile soil for further journey of the soul, preventing them from the eternal fall. Grace and mercy of God will be a protecting wall for such souls. A life with pure mind will be in peace and tranquillity. In the Christian way of life, one comes to know that the holy Eucharist; the centre of Christian life is the source of peace and tranquillity. It is with the blood of Christ that everything is cleansed (cf. Heb. 9:22) and made holy. Christ alone is the great priest over the house of God and can put the laws of the temple in the hearts and write them on the minds (cf. Heb. 10:16) It is Jesus who renews each one with a new heart that becomes something greater than the material temple (cf. Mt 12:6). Such lives with a renewed heart in Christ becomes a living temple of glory and holiness. They will not be static but a temple with a wheel that can roll away all the disgraces and carried anywhere according to the wishes of Christ. St. Therese of child Jesus says that "It is not to remain in a golden ciborium that God comes to us each day from heaven; it's to find another heaven, infinitely dearer to Him than the first: the heaven of our soul, made to His image, the living temple of the adorable Trinity!"[223]

Having a constant touch in life with the altar of Christ and the Holy Eucharist is to have a unique touch with God Who comes again. It is the source of divine power, wisdom and love. This altar is not only of a God who was sacrificed or dead, but also the eternal One, and the living God. The interior eye to see wisdom behind every wind is given to the one who bind oneself to the altar of Christ. They will be able to analyse their life by sitting beside the one who is seated at the east gate of their living temple. In Him alone can find meaning for all the winds that comes to them. Because He is the one who withstood all the destructive winds by directing and

223 Allen–Johan Bergstrom (ed.), *Carmel and the Eucharist Climbing the Mountain, The Carmelite Journey*, (Saint Albert's Press & Edizioni Carmelitne, United Kingdom, 2010) p. 313.

transforming them by the merit of his sacrificial blood with which He could reign over the world and whole cosmos.

The life-giving water and the river flowing from the altar of the renewed temple in the book of Ezekiel symbolically represents the fertility and life-giving power.[224] As the water from the altar of the renewed temple shows its effects throughout the year by growing life giving trees, the water that flows from the side of Christ whose sacrifice is offered at the altar, works miraculously in the life of a believer. A soul that is renewed in Christ and grows at the side of the sacred and loving heart of Christ by being budded in Him (cf. Jn 15:5, 16) will never have anything that is cursed in it, but it will be a tree that holds the throne of God (cf. Rev 22:3, Ezek 43:7). The water that flows from Christ cleanses, purifies, heals and gives freshness in life. This stream from the altar or the life flowing from the Eucharistic Jesus enables persons to live a virtuous life, and the souls get healed from their wounded feelings, freed of its actions and passions in which it was formerly occupied or drowned in. Christ who comes again to anoint the souls who are renewed with the spirit of repentance finds them at His altar every day and empowers and fills them with divine power and the soul is clothed with holiness, grandeur, strength, power, delight and glory that ever shines.

Conclusion

In the third chapter we were trying to build a new and a living temple in Christ who is the corner stone of the living temple. If spoken in terms of the structure and construction for any building, first thing needed is forming a basic structure and in the second stage is settling the materials available for it. In the first and second chapters, we made sure of it by recognizing the basic structure of our self and how the theories and principles of Christ can help us to perfect this structured life. Now in the third stage made an analysis for the real construction of the temple by recognizing how this temple can be built in Christ.

---

224 Lawrence Boadt, "Ezekiel", in Brown R. E., Fitzmyer J. A.– Murphy R. E. (ed.), *The New Jerome Biblical Commentary* (Bangalore: Theological Publications in India, 2004) p. 327.

In the first stage of this construction of the living temple, we get assured of the living aspect; the presence of God in us. As the presence of God makes a temple along with its rituals, the human soul with the presence of God along with its virtuous and living sacrificial life is characteristically explained. Another aspect of the temple is its ritual sacrifices performed in a temple. Considering the living temple how the sacrifices are done? As a living temple the sacrifices must also be living sacrifices. It is performed through the virtues of faith, hope and love. The initial step is of the slight sacrifices and mortifications done with a spirit of repentant heart.

The three stages of elevation of holiness explained with three progressive stages in relation with Christ as, servant, friend and filial or bridal growth is a structure within the structure of a living temple. The rooting through humility is also an important element in the building up of the temple in Christ. From the first chapter onwards, the relevance of faith, hope and love and the application of it with each faculties of intellect, memory and will is mentioned. In this chapter also brings out the relevance of faith in liberating oneself through accepting and loving oneself, acts of prayer in faith that becomes the channels of grace, relevance of safeguarding oneself through holiness, and growth in the recognition of God's works of liberation through the winds or the experiences of life that changes the shape of one's whole structure.

Confirming oneself through hope in the redemptive love of Christ that widens the realm of hope as it progresses is explained in the part that analyses the confirmation through hope. It focuses on the point that Christ is the central source of our hope and from where can flow energy to live our life and who can fix our memory to the eternal rewards and promises without being discontented in life. This part also enhances the point that by looking at Christ who is the replica of God's mind, one can possess wisdom that is in Christ, where the fullness of God dwells and in whom we can find meaning for our life. This part also becomes a pointer for us to recognize how a man's intellect becomes a channel of God's revelation by entering into a life of solitude and silence in order to grow in relation with God. Also, emphasis is made on the memory that is centred on Christ as a memory that retrieved from all the worries and cares that are unwanted and a memory that will experience the lasting peace and rest in God and eternity. The changes of a life rooted with hope in God in its realm of will are also discussed here. Virtue of hope transforms its mere activities as sacred and sacrificial at the altar of its will which is purified with divine wisdom and values of Christ.

The concluding part of this chapter comes out with a message that the soul that is transformed with divine love is established its will in love at the service of God for the good of oneself and for the glory of God. It also brings out how a penitent heart can be found in Christ who is seated at the east gate of life, in whom can unite and reconcile the lost ones and broken relations. The analysis done with the Gilgal and the message derived from it with the relevance of the altar of Christ becomes a source of strength to submit oneself to the sacramental grace of Christ. The concluding part of this chapter leads the inner journey to a life-giving river that flows from this altar of Christ which becomes a channel of virtuous life where a soul is transformed to be a temple of God in Christ.

General Conclusion

While journeying to the inner sanctuary, the soul has to face many tests and conquer many temptations but along with it receives the gift to acquire the three vital graces from God, the grace to be clothed with the power, wisdom and love; the very nature and the likeness of God. Just as the whole of Israel found refuge and protection in the holy name of God, the power one share will be the power of the name of God. Amidst all the powers, the power of love is unending and the soul gets life continued with it not from anywhere, but from the altar of Christ who loved until death, yet still alive to love again. A hope that is rooted in Christ is a hope that cannot find climax in love and life alone but in renewing and rejuvenating them. For Christ's death was not a finishing point of his love, but a means to start his love in the world with new forms and means. This is what he meant while saying "Destroy this temple, and in three days I will raise it up" (Jn 2:19). Whole aim of Christ was to rise again and make others to rise up. One who journeys along with Christ to the inner sanctuary of self will possess this risen experience from one's own rotten and dead self. Our discussion on the theme 'From Glory to Holy' provides an inner journey with the effect of God's glory and holiness from one's exterior senses to the inner most self as well as a transformed journey of reverse flow of innermost self to the outer self. But, at this time, the centre of the self will be the altar of Christ, who began life from His own sacrificial table. Repairing our own self while approaching the great sanctuary of Christ is an inevitable need. This is what Christ demanded to St. Francis of Assisi "repair my ruined

Church" which simultaneously expressed a symbolism of renewing the true spirit of the church.[225] In order to repair, one needs to check the whole structure of a building. The reparation gets easy when it is done with a structurally ordered manner. As "the Lord's Table is getting despised" (Mal 1:7) the reparation is considering the despised selves while approaching the altar of Christ without forgetting our greatness and holiness.

In order to fix one's whole faculties of self into a central focus - Christ, an understanding of the structural elements of the self is necessary. For this, it is found that the analysis done by St. John of the cross, on the structure of man is worth noticing. According to John of the Cross, human self is structured in three operative systems. These three parts are the lower part of the soul, higher part of the soul, and the centre of the soul.

As this chapter is completely based on the teachings of John of the Cross, in the culminating point also the saint does not fail to be apt in edifying the souls to enter into open mysticism and learn to inculcate oneself from everything that one encounter with a mystical dimension. In short, for a soul who travels with God, the whole of creation proclaims the wisdom and mysteries of God and for such souls everything will be symbolical just as the saint looked at the human self and whole cosmos. This chapter becomes a genuine foundation for a human self with a structural foundation where the coming chapter can continue the life structure for its further journey to the inner most centre.

The Structure of the renewed temple of Prophet Ezekiel in the second chapter also reveals that; just like the steps in the temple and the invitation of the guide from outer court to the inner sanctuary, our life journey is an inward journey with steps of progression. It is an entry from outer court to the inner sanctuary. Instead of focussing on others or external realities, it is always successful to look at oneself and talk to one's own intellect and conscience along with divine knowledge as our guide. And after an understanding of one's own self

---

225 Leost Keeprath, *Francis Assisi*, (Viani Printings, Cochin, 1984) pp. 74, 117; J. Regis Armstrong, Wayne J. A Hellmann (ed.), *The Saint, Francis of Assisi: Early Documents*, (New City Press, New York) V. 1, pp. 243 ff.

with a structural outlook in the first chapter, the structure division of the renewed temple unveils more features of our life structure with more clarity. The structure division of human self as lower part and higher part is very apt for now to recognize how the living temple of our human self is divided with lower part as 'footstool' of Yahweh to reside, work and highest part as the 'Throne' to rest for ever.

The renewed temple with its representation on the life of prophet himself just before applying it to the people of Israel is also a replica of a spiritual life centred on self. The life of prophet which was centred on the holiness of Yahweh and the eager desire to retain the holy Name of Yahweh which was profaned by the false witnessing of his own people recalls the relevance of a holy life. In the vision of the renewed temple and inner life of a person the effort of a small synchronization happens with the previous chapter as well as with the following chapter which reveals how the human life is formed to be the living temple. From here onwards, the themes are more corresponding, the aspect of mountain, east gate and the cross of Christ, the wall around the temple area, the steps, the prince, gate ways and entrances, offerings, measuring reeds etc. are placed with its own new meaning as they are found. The analysis done on the structure of a living temple with the support of John's spirituality and also from the renewed temple vision of Ezekiel is an honest effort to derive the spiritual nourishments from these complementary sources.

As the person progress in the journey, a growth and deepening in the three theological virtues happens. While leaving from the sanctuary to the outer court, the soul is vested with new garments of virtues and the explanations by John for identifying them with distinct colours provide still deeper knowledge for travellers in their uncertainties. The invitation of prince to dine with soul in the temple is also very important to think. Here, with all the characteristics of the renewed temple of Ezekiel, Christ the prince of peace has entered into the living temple of human souls, and He alone is the only delight of souls who really search God with all the sweat and blood of life. He alone can quench the thirst of wearied hearts to find consolation with a God who suffered the same thirst and weariness, yet sufficient and rich in Himself now to feed the whole humanity. He is the life-giving tree and source of living water and the one who is budded in Him will bear the same fruit and will be a channel from the main spring in the living temple.

The Centrality of Christ is focussed at this point. This part is an attempt to enhance how Christ and the attributes, mysteries, judgments and virtues of God in Christ are symbolized and expressed in many ways and forms throughout the writings of John and how it can be useful for souls who are in an inner journey. This path of wisdom to Christ is a saving window through which one can gaze in and out of oneself and conform to the will of God by conforming oneself to the will of Christ. This finding also reaches to the point of understanding that how Christ's love and wisdom enable souls to find consolation amidst all the trials, tribulations, distress, dryness and miseries and how it is not oppressive amidst its nothingness, weakness and sufferings.

Towards the end we get also a vivid picture of how a soul who reaches to the inmost centre will look like. It will have the characteristic of a dove which will be simple, meek, without gall, bright and loving eyes that can look at God as He is and look at oneself and others through the same glance. It speaks of the relevance of the Cross of Christ in order to get purified of one's natural passions, appetites, emotions, distress, etc., while getting restored of its genuine nature. For the peaceful flow of a life-giving river, this part also emphasises to judge and evaluate oneself only with the measuring reed and cord, Christ the crucified. For one who wish to gain wisdom needs to join with Christ's mind and make it pass through the gate-the Cross of Christ. The above said analysis naturally leads to an invitation to be a living temple of God through the presence of God within.

The third chapter provides a vivid picture of a living temple in Christ without losing its structured elements along with God's presence in three distinctive forms such as in way of essence, grace and affection. The further narration of three stages of spiritual progression in three stages through liberation by faith from the sensual world, confirmation through the grace of hope at the interior faculties and restoration through love at the centre of the soul with its constitutive parts of outer court, inner court and temple proper supports us to build a true living temple in Christ.

With the first and second chapters, we were finding our own life structure with the supportive offsets that sustains them: the faith, hope and love. By finding our own structure and making an inner journey by ourselves without a guide to interpret our life may make the journey still and struck on the way. Because though we are created in the image and likeness of God, our life structure is distorted and deformed by sins, imperfections and weaknesses. But, a journey to our own self with a person who is perfect with a life structure and armed with the power and wisdom and good will of love can reform or reshape and renew us to the best and suitable structure. And now Christ Jesus is surely a perfect guide for this task. Anyone who travels with Christ Jesus will find an extraordinary inner power to restore one's life and they will surely share the light of Christ as He became the light of the world. Following Christ is not a failure, but we will become successful by possessing a perfect self-structure with a perfect intellect, memory and will that enable us to win the interior castle or inner sanctuary of God within or own self.

An intellect with divine knowledge is a strong support to take off an inner journey and convictions from this journey experience in Christ becomes the way that leads us to the seeds of truth within the inner sanctuary of soul. Truth is a hidden treasure deeply dug and preserved within the centre of the soul as the presence of God in essence. Anyone who possesses a true conscience from the Spirit of God will be able to read the truths from their own life scroll. This was the vision of Job who could possess this truth within and read himself with a true conscience (cf. Job 42:5-6). Such knowledge of God is thwarting for many. All of us desire of a God who comforts us with all our deep-rooted ignorance that hinder us from reading oneself. We are in search of a God who provides us everything that we require yet fail to reach Him by amending our way to within. "Thus, says the Lord: Stand at the crossroads, and look, and ask for the ancient paths, where the good way lies" (Jer 6:16). Way to God is inward and the faces of Mountain[226] in this ascend is our intellect, memory and will which are also the crossroads for us to look and enquire of our old ways. By repairing or refining them we

226 John of the Cross, S.C. stz.19:4, p. 486.

will find the good way that lies hidden behind the dust or ashes. "Amend your ways and your doings and let me dwell with you in this place" (Jer 7:3). This amending is nothing but being true to the conscience of oneself and of others up to a stage where we reach we are in want of "nothing" that makes us submissive to the ultimate divine presence and Will.

In short, according to John, a person is only a vessel which becomes a channel for receiving grace from God and if one possesses a consciousness clear and pure like crystal, a temple is formed for God's indwelling. If Christ is the temple provider and the gate to enter in, we shouldn't turn back to any other gate but travel ahead with wisdom of Christ in knowing God and oneself and it is great to be in the temple of the Lord, except in the requirement of the needy. Let us not be deceptive with the words: "This is the temple of the LORD, the temple of the Lord, the temple of the Lord" (Jer 7:4), that leads us to waist our life time and of our generations to build the temples that are perishable while forgetting to renew the ruined temples within our own self and around us. This is the fact that Jesus promised to worship God first at the mountain top of oneself in spirit and truth before arriving to the temple outside.

Bibliography

Books

Allers Rudolf, *Successful Error: A Critical Study of Freudian Psychoanalysis* (Sheed and Ward, London 1941).

Allers Rudolf, *Self-Improvement*, (Benizger Brothers, New York, 1939).

Amaladoss Michael, *Creative Conflict*, (St. Pauls, Bombay, 1995).

Antony D. John, *Family Counselling*, (Anugraha Publications, Dindigul, Tamil Nadu, 2005).

Arraj James, *St. John of the Cross and Dr. C. G. Jung, Christian Mysticism in the Light of Jungian Psychology*, (Inner Growth Books, Chiloquin OR, U. S. A, 1988).

Arraj J., *From John of the Cross to Us: The Story of a 400 Years Long Misunderstanding and What it Means for the Future of Christian Mysticism*, (Inner Growth Books, Chiloquin OR, U. S. A, 1999).

Baker Lynne Rudder, *Persons and Bodies, A Constitution View*, (Cambridge Universities Press, Cambridge, 2000).

Barret E. Boyd, *Strength of Will*, (P. J. Kennedy Sons, New York, 1915).

Benedict XVI, *Verbum Domini*, (Carmel International Publishing House, Trivandrum, 2011).

Benedict XVI, *Spe Salvi (On Christian Hope)*, (Libreria Editrice Vaticana, Citta del Vaticano, 2007).

Bergstrom Allen–Johan, (ed.), "*Teresa of Jesus" Climbing the Mountain, The Carmelite Journey*, (Saint Albert's Press & Edizioni Carmelitne, United Kingdom, 2010).

Bergson Henri, *Matter and Memory*, (George Alllen and Unwin, London, 1910).

Bethelheim Bruno, *Freud and Man's Soul*, (Fontana Paperbacks, London, 1982).

Bourne Peter, *St. John of the Cross and the Dark Night*, (Wenzel Press, 1993).

Blommestijn H., Huls J., Waaijman K., *The Foots of Love: John of the Cross as Guide in the Wilderness*, (Leuven, Peters, 2000).

Bourne Peter, *St. John of the Cross and the Dark Night,* Wenzel Press, CA,1993).

Burrows R., *Ascent to Love: Spiritual Teachings of St. John of the Cross*, (St. Paul's Publications, Bombay, 1990).

Castell Alburey, *Self in Philosophy*, (The Macmillan Company, Collier Macmillan Ltd. 1965).

Carretto Carlo, *In Search of the Beyond*, (Daughters of St. Paul, Bombay, 1976).

Catechism of the Catholic Church, Libreria Editrice Vaticana, (Image Doubleday, New York, 1995).

Chakiathe Peter, *The Art of Unveiling the Spirit*, (Carmel International Publishing House, Trivandrum, 2015).

Cheyne T. K.- Sutherland J., *Encyclopaedia Biblica, A Dictionary of the Bible*, (Adam & Charles Black, MCMXIV 1914).

Congar Yves M. J., *Mystery of the Temple: The Manner of God's Presence to His Creatures from Genesis to the Apocalypse*, (Sheed and Ward, New York, 1958).

Collings Ross, *John of the Cross, The Way of the Christian Mystics*, (The Liturgical Press, Collegeville, Minnesota, 1990).

Crowe H. John, *You can Master Life*, (Better Yourself Books, Bangalore, 1973).

Cristiani Leon, *John of the Cross; Prince of Mystical Theology*, (Doubleday, New York, 1962).

Cummins Norbert, *An Introduction to St. John of the Cross*, (Darlington Carmel, [Private Circulation only]).

Dicken E. W. Trueman, *The Crucible of Love, A Study of the Mysticism of St. Teresa of Jesus and St. John of the Cross*, (Sheed and Ward, New York, 1963).

Donoghue O' Noel, *Mystics for Our Time*, (Michael Glazier, Wilmington, Delaware, 1989).

Doohan L., *The Contemporary Challenge of John of the Cross: An Introduction to His Life and Teaching*, (CPC, Trivandrum,1998).

D'souza Gregory, *Spiritual Doctrine of St. John of the Cross Doctor of the Church,* (Dhyanavana Publications, Bangalore, 2016).

________, *Contemplative Formation*, (Dhyanavana Publications, Bangalore, 2013).

________, *Mystical Wisdom*, (Dhyanavana Publications, Bangalore, 2016).

________, *Spiritual Direction in Prayer and Contemplation with St. John of the Cross as Guide*, (Dhyanavana Publications, Bangalore, 2016).

D'souza V. Rudolf, *The Bhagavadgita and St. John of the Cross*, Gujarat Sahitya Prakash, Gujarat, 1997.

Dijk H. J.Van, *Ezekiel's Prophecy on Tyre*, Pontifical Biblical Institute, Roma, 1968.

Doherty Joseph F. & Stepheson William (ed.), *Inward Journey*, (Harcourt Brace Jovanovich, Inc, New York, 1973).

Douglas M. Julie, *Spiritual Discernment: The Locutions of St. Teresa of Avila and St. John of the Cross*, (Carmel in the World-1995) V. XXXIV, N. 3.

Edward F. Siegman, *The Book of Ezechiel*, (Bible Series 30, Paulist Press, New York, 1961).

________, *The Book of Ezechiel*, (Bible Series 31, Paulist Press, New York, 1961).

Egan D. Harvey, *An Anthology of Christian Mysticism*, (The Liturgical Press, Minnesota, 1996).

Ellis Albert, *Anger: How to Live With and Without It*, (Jaico Publishing House, Bombay, 1977).

Fastiggi L. Robert, Koterski W. Joseph (et.al.), (ed.), *New Catholic Encyclopaedia*, The Catholic University of America, (Gale Cengage learning, Washington D. C, 2013), V. 2.

Ferriere Adolphe, *Psychological Types: And the Stages of Man's Development*, (William Heinemann Ltd., London 1958).

Francis De Sales, (tr.) Vincent Kerns, *The Love of God*, (S. F. S. Publications, Asian Trading Corporation, Bangalore, 1982).

Gabriel, *John of the Cross: Doctor of Divine Love and Contemplation*, (Cork, The Mercier Publication, 1952).

Georgia Harkness, *Mysticism its Meaning and Message* (Abingdon Press, Nashville, New York 1973).

Gelpi L. Donald, *Charism and Sacrament*, (SPCK, London 1977).

Green B. Joel, *"Humanity – Created, Restored, Transformed, Embodied", Rethinking Human Nature*, (William B. Eerdmans Publishing Company, Cambridge, U. K, 2011), 271-294.

Guttenplan Samuel, *Mind's Landscape: An Introduction to the Philosophy of Mind*, (Blackwell Publishers, Oxford, 2000).

Hamilton E., *The Voice of the Spirit: Spirituality of John of the Cross*, Longman & Todd, London, 1976).

Hastings James, *Dictionary of the Bible*, (Edinburgh, T & T Clark).

Heinisch Paul – G. H. William, *Theology of the Old Testament*, (Minnesota, The Liturgical Press, 1955).

________, *History of the Old Testament*, (Minnesota, The Liturgical Press,1952).

Hess E. Valerie & Arnold M. Lane, *Life of the Body*, (St. Paul's Mumbai, 2013).

Howells E., *John of the Cross and Teresa of Avila: Mystical Knowing and Selfhood*, (The Cross Road Publishing House, New York, 2002).

Iglesias Yolanda & Salvatore Putzu, *The Promise, An Introduction to the Old Testament*, (Word and Life Publications, Philippines, 1996).

Janen J. Gerald, *"Job" Interpretation, A Bible Commentary for Teaching and Preaching,* (John Knox Press, Atlanta, 1985).

John of The Cross, *Dark Night of the Soul,* (Peers E. Allison (tr.), Image Books, New York, 2005).

Keiran Kavanaugh, Otilio Rodriguez, (tr.), *St. John of the Cross, Collected Works* (Carmel International Publishing House, Trivandrum, Kerala, 2006).

John of The Cross, *Ascend of Mount Carmel,* (Peers E. Allison, (tr.), Image Books, New York, 1962).

John of The Cross, *Spiritual Canticle,* (Peers E. Allison, (tr.), Image Books, New York, 1961).

John of The Cross, *Living Flame of Love,* (Peers E. Allison, (tr.), Image Books, New York, 1962).

John Paul II, *Ecclesia in America,* (Apostolic Exhortations), (Carmel International Publishing House, Trivandrum, 2005).

John Paul II, *Evangelium Vitae,* (Encyclical), (Carmel International Publishing House, Trivandrum, 2005).

Kavanaugh Kieran, *John of the Cross; Doctor of Light and Love,* (The Crossroad Publishing Company, New York, 1999).

Kellyp. H, *Biblical Hebrew, An Introductory Grammar,* (William B. Eerdmans Publishing Company Grand Rapids, Michigan, 1992).

Kee Howard Clark, *Medicine, Miracle, & Magic in New Testament Times,* (Cambridge University Press, Cambridge, 1990).

Kurisumkal Martin Joseph, *The Purification of Memory According to St. John of the Cross,* (Universidad Pontificia, Comillas Madrid, Facultad De Teologia Instituto De Espiritualidad, 2011).

L. Ryken, J. C. Whilhoit, L. Tremper, *Dictionary of Biblical Imagery, An Encyclopaedic Exploration of the Images, Symbols, Motifs, Metaphors, Figures of Speech and Literary Patterns of the Bible* (InterVarsity Press, USA, 1998).

Leon Philip, *Body, Mind and Spirit,* (SCM Press, London, 1948).

Mathew Iain, *The Impact of God; Soundings from St. John of the Cross,* (Hodder & Stoughton Ltd., London, 2010).

Manasseh Michael, *Searchers for God, The Evolution of an Ideal,* (Lisieux Offset Printers, Palluruthy, Kochi, 2004).

Mary O' Driscoll (ed.) *Catherine of Siena; Passion for the Truth Compassion for Humanity* (New City Press, New York, 1993).

Mein Andrew, *Ezekiel and the Ethics of Exile*, (Oxford University Press, 2006).

Mc Caffrey James, *Captive Flames*, Veritas Publications, Ireland, 2005.

Mickelsen Berkeley A., *Interpreting the Bible*, (WM. B. Erdmans Publishing Company Grand Rapids, Michigan,1985).

M. V. Antony, *The Mystical Dimension of Priestly Formation Today*, (SFS Publications, Bangalore, 2019).

Muto Susan, *John of the Cross for Today: The Dark Night*, (Ave Maria Publications, Indiana, 1994).

________, *John of the Cross for Today: The Ascent*, (Ave Maria Publications, Indiana, 1991).

Nogar J. Raymond, *The Wisdom of Evolution*, (A Mentor–Omega Book, The New American Library, New York, 1966).

Panakal Justin, *Saint Teresa of Avila Forever our Contemporary*, (Jyotir Dharma Publications, Kalamassery, 2016).

Pacho Eulogio, *The Art of Reaching God According to St. John of the Cross*, (Mulloor Augustine (tr.), Jyothir Dhara Publications, Kalamassery 1990).

Ralph Alexander, *Ezekiel*, (Moody Press, Chicago, 1978).

Rosmini Antonio, (tr.), Cleary Denis, Watson Terence, *Essence of the Human Soul*, (Rosmini House, Durham, 1989) V. 1.

________, (tr.), Cleary Denis, Watson Terence, *Development of the Human Soul*, (Rosmini House, Durham, 1989) V. 2.

Siegman F. Edward, *The Book of Ezechiel*, (Paulist Press, New York).

Sherbok Dan Cohn, *The Hebrew Bible* (Cassel, New York, 1996).

Smart Ninian, "Hinduism", Philip L. Quinn , Charles Taliaferro (ed.) *A Companion to Philosophy of Religion*, (Blackwell Publishers, Oxford, 2000).

Tanguerey Adolphe, *The Spiritual Life A Treatise on Ascetical and Mystical Theology*, (Society of St. John the Evangelist, Tournai, Belgium, 1930).

Teresa of Avila, *Interior Castle*, (Peers E. Allison, (tr.), Image Books, New York, 1972).

Tran Hai, *The Dark Night and Its Pastoral Applications in Clinical Settings* (CIW-2011), V. L. N. 2.

Wagner, Joseph F., *Catholic Biblical Encyclopaedia, Old Testament*, (I. N. C Publishers, New York City, 1956).

Wakefield S. Gordon, *A Dictionary of Christian Spirituality*, (SCM Press Ltd, London, 1983).

Watkin E. I., *Bow in the Clouds*, (Sheed Ward, London, 1931).

Winzen Damasus, *Pathways in Scripture*, (Word of Life, Michigan, 1976).

Witherup D. Ronald, *The Bile Companion*, (Claretian Publications, Bangalore, 1999).

Woods Richard, *Mysticism and Prophecy*, (Orbis books, New York, 1998).

Zerafa Paul Peter, *The Wisdom of God in the Book of Job*, (Herder, Roma, 1978).

Zimmerli Walther, *Ezekiel 1, A Commentary on the Book of the Prophet Ezekiel* (Fortress Press, Philadelphia, 1977).

_________, *Ezekiel 2, A Commentary on the Book of the Prophet Ezekiel*, (Fortress Press, Philadelphia, 1983).

Articles

Acharuparambil Daniel, "Advaita mysticism vis-a-vis the teaching of St. John of the Cross", in Panakal Justin, (ed.), *St. John of the Cross, Studies on His Life, Doctrine and Time*, (Jyothir Dhara Publications, Kalamassery, 1991) p.104.

Lawrence Boadt, "Ezekiel", in Brown R. E., Fitzmyer J. A.– Murphy R. E. (ed.), *The New Jerome Biblical Commentary* (Theological Publications in India, Bangalore, 2004) pp. 326-328.

Blenkinsopp Joseph, "Ezekiel", *Interpretation – A Bible Commentary for Teaching and Preaching* (John Knox Press, Louisville, 1990), pp. 201-239.

Boyle Brian, "Holiness has a Shape: The place of the Altar in Ezekiel's visionary plan of Sacral Space (Ez. 43:1-12, 13-17, 18-27)" in *Australian Biblical Review,* 2008-09 Vol. 57, pp. 1-21.

Chowning Daniel, "Free to Love: Negation in the Doctrine of John of the Cross", in Payne Steven, (ed.), *Carmelite Studies, John of the Cross: Conferences and Essays by Members of the Institute of Carmelite Studies and Others,* ICS Publications, Washington, D.C. 1992), pp. 29-47.

Culligan Kevin, "Qualities of A Good Guide: Spiritual Direction in John of the Cross's Letters", in *Carmelite Studies, John of the Cross: Conferences and Essays by Members of the Institute of Carmelite Studies and Others,* Payne Steven, (ed.), ICS Publications, Washington, D. C. 1992) p. 70.

Dodd Michael, "John of the Cross: The Person, His Times, His Writings", in Payne Steven, (ed.), *Carmelite Studies, John of the Cross: Conferences and Essays by Members of the Institute of Carmelite Studies and others,* ICS Publications, Washington D. C. 1992) pp. 7-28.

Hardy P. Richard, "Embodied love in John of the Cross", in Payne Steven, (ed.), *Carmelite Studies, John of the Cross: Conferences and Essays by Members of the Institute of Carmelite Studies and Others,* (ICS Publications, Washington, D.C. 1992) p. 129.

Jordan Regis, "Jesus Christ in the Writings of John of the Cross", in Payne Steven, (ed.), *Carmelite Studies, John of the Cross: Conferences and Essays by Members of the Institute of Carmelite Studies and others,* (ICS Publications, Washington, D. C. 1992) pp. 98-108.

Karakunnel George, "St. John of the Cross and the life of Faith", in Panakal Justin, (ed.), *St. John of the Cross, Studies on His Life, Doctrine and Time,* (JyothirDhara Publications, Kalamassery, 1991) pp. 73-80.

Kavanaugh Kieran, "Faith and the Experience of God in the University town of Baeza", in Payne Steven, (ed.), *Carmelite*

Studies, John of the Cross: Conferences and Essays by Members of the Institute of Carmelite Studies and Others, (ICS Publications, Washington D. C. 1992) pp. 48-64.

Koottanal G. Benny, "Salesian Eucharistic Theology Anthropological Perspectives", in *Indian Journal of Spirituality*, (S.F.S Publication, Bangalore, 2012) V. XXV, 2. p. 136.

Lozano M. John, "John of the Cross: A Radical Reinterpretation of Discipleship", in Payne Steven, (ed.), *Carmelite Studies VI, John of the Cross: Conferences and Essays by Members of The Institute of Carmelite Studies and others*, (ICS Publications, Washington D. C. 1992) p. 123-140.

Moulton J. Wilfrid, "Glory", in *Dictionary of the Bible*, (T & T Clark & Charles Scribner's Sons, Edinburgh, 2, 1963) p. 331-332.

Mueller J. R. & Robinson S. E., "Apocryphon of Ezekiel" in *The Old Testament Pseudepigrapha*, Vol. 1, (Doubleday, New York, 1983), 487-495.

Muilenburg J., "Ezekiel", in Mathew Black & Rowley H. H., (ed.), *Peake's Commentary on the Bible*, (Routledge, Taylor & Francis Group, London, 2001) pp. 570-588.

Mulloor Augustine, "St. John of the Cross and Contemporary Man", in Panakal Justin, (ed.), *St. John of the Cross, Studies on His Life, Doctrine and Time*, (Jyothir Dhara Publications, Kalamassery, 1991) p. 44-52.

Palliparambil Jacob, "Theological life: a Programme for Spiritual Life", in Panakal Justin, (ed.), *St. John of the Cross, Studies on His Life, Doctrine and Time*, (Jyothir Dhara Publications, Kalamassery, 1991) pp. 64-72.

Panakal Justin, "John of the Cross, A Saint for All", in Panakal Justin, (ed.), *St. John of the Cross, Studies on His Life, Doctrine and Time*, (Jyothir Dhara Publications, Kalamassery, 1991) pp. 1-27.

Paul VI, "Preparation for Christmas", in *The Teachings of Pope Paul VI*, (Libreria Editrice Vaticana, 1976) p. 144.

Puthur Bosco, "Christology of St. John of the Cross", in Panakal Justin, (ed.), *St. John of the Cross, Studies on His Life, Doctrine and Time*, (Jyothir Dhara Publications, Kalamassery, 1991) p. 53-64

Rebeiro Manuel, "The Imagery of Faith "Bride" and the "Bridegroom" in the writings of St. John of the Cross", in Panakal Justin, (ed.), *St. John of the Cross, Studies on His Life, Doctrine and Time*, (Jyothir Dhara Publications, Kalamassery, 1991) p. 81-100.

Read Denis, "John of the Cross for Carpenters the Ordinary way of the Dark Night of Faith", in (Payne Steven, (ed.), *Carmelite Studies, John of the Cross: Conferences and Essays by Members of the Institute of Carmelite Studies and others*, (ICS Publications, Washington, D.C. 1992) p. 88.

Smith J., Acworth A., Hemer C. J "Wind", in Mary Gladstone (et.al) (ed.) *The Illustrated Bible Dictionary*, (InterVarsity Press, Tyndale House Publishers, UK, 1980) p. 1647.

Soskice Janet Martin, "Imago Dei and Sexual Difference: Toward an Eschatological Anthropology" in *Rethinking Human Nature*, (William B. Eerdmans Publishing Company, Cambridge, U. K, 2011) p. 295-306.

Spittler R. P, "Testament of Job" in *The Old Testament Pseudepigrapha*, Vol. 1, Doubleday, New York, 1983) p. 829-868.

Sullivan John, "How Is It God Loves Us? A Homily for St. John of the Cross", in Payne Steven (ed.), Carmelite Studies, John of the Cross: Conferences and Essays by Members of the Institute of Carmelite Studies and others, (ICS Publications, Washington D. C. 1992) pp. 1-6.

Sullivan J. Emmanuel, "Mary and the Holy Spirit in the writings of St. John of the Cross", in Payne Steven (ed.), *Carmelite Studies, John of the Cross: Conferences and Essays by Members of the Institute of Carmelite Studies and others*, (ICS Publications, Washington D. C. 1992) pp. 109-122.

Thachil Jose, "The Indian Mysticism and the Mysticism of St. John of the Cross", in Panakal Justin, (ed.), St. John of the Cross, Studies on his life, doctrine and Time, (Jyothir Dhara Publications, Kalamassery, 1991) pp. 124-133.

W. W. Battershall, *"Ezekiel"* in Joseph S. Exell, (ed.), The Biblical Illustrator, (Baker Book House, Grand Rapids, Michigan, 1977) pp. 504-506.